W9-ADV-874

THE BEST IS YET TO BE

DISCOVERING THE SECRET TO A CREATIVE,
HAPPY RETIREMENT

MIKE BELLAH, PH.D.

 PRESS

CANYON, TX

Copyright © 2019 by Mike Bellah

All rights reserved.

No part of this book may be reproduced in any form or by any electronic or mechanical means, including information storage and retrieval systems, without written permission from the author, except for the use of brief quotations in a book review.

Unless otherwise noted, scripture quotations are taken from the New American Standard Bible® (NASB), Copyright © 1960, 1962, 1963, 1968, 1971, 1972, 1973, 1975, 1977, 1995 by The Lockman Foundation. Used by permission. www.Lockman.org

Scripture notated NKJV is taken from the New King James Version®. Copyright © 1982 by Thomas Nelson. Used by permission. All rights reserved.

THE HOLY BIBLE, NEW INTERNATIONAL VERSION®, NIV® Copyright © 1973, 1978, 1984, 2011 by Biblica, Inc.® Used by permission. All rights reserved worldwide.

Published by BestYears Press, Canyon, TX, USA

V 6/17/20

DEDICATION

To Hidden Falls Ranch
— where it all began

CONTENTS

Grow old along with me!
The best is yet to be,
the last of life,
for which the first was made.
—Robert Browning

FOREWORD

For over 50 years, Americans of a certain age have been told that the happiest people are able to quit working completely, as early as possible, and spend the rest of their days in an upscale retirement community. And we have been told, mostly by those who have investments to sell, that the key to this bliss is money saved, lots of money.

What if I told you money is not the number one requirement for a happy retirement? And what if focusing solely on money leads not to Nirvana, but to frustration and depression (if you don't have enough) or frustration and boredom (if you have plenty)?

What if there's something else, something that costs nothing, but something that will supply all you need (including the funds) for what could be the happiest years of your life?

And what if I told you that research shows you can do more than just get by in your later years? What if it's possible to thrive, to have a healthy body and sharp mind, close friends, new adventures, meaningful service to others (including grandkids), a better-than-anticipated income and more joy than you thought possible this side of 60?

Mike Bellah
Canyon, Texas
June, 2019

THE BEST IS YET TO BE

INTRODUCTION
THE APARTMENT FLOOR

"You're no good. You're no good." My words, mixed with some embarrassing tears, sounded childish and vaguely familiar. They brought memories of what psychologist Philip Zimbardo called "past negatives," traumatic experiences from years gone by, forgotten during good times, but all too real when life turns hard.

It was a sunny Saturday morning in June 2016, just a few weeks after I had taught my last English class at Amarillo College. I was lying face down on the floor of a small efficiency apartment supplied by the generosity of a friend (we had sold our home of 36 years and were mid-way in the process of building a new one). And I was in tears. Literally. Not one given to such outbursts, I, also, was ashamed. Not because of the tears but of what I thought one of the stupidest decisions of my 67 years. But I'm getting ahead of myself.

I had just gotten off the phone with a friend who told me why my usually upbeat loan officer had appeared so worried. "He's afraid the committee won't approve your loan," were her words. What? Six months before I had sailed through the preapproval. And now I had more assets than then—a 401K, monthly teacher retirement payments, equity in some rental properties. Everything but—she finished my thought for me —"You no longer have your professor's paycheck."

It was my first lesson in retirement economics. Bankers don't care about net worth; bankers care about cash flow. And my cash flow—the money I had to spend each month—had taken a hit. A big hit.

Funny how quickly things change. At the end of May, I had stood at the top of Atalaya Mountain overlooking Santa Fe and Northern New Mexico's beautiful Rio Grande Valley. There, I felt like the luckiest guy on the planet. Surrounded by students and colleagues with whom I had experienced some of my happiest times, the climb was to be a capstone, a fitting conclusion to life as a college professor and the beginning of a happy retirement.

It wasn't just the elevation in Texas that was lower now. My feelings, my hopes, were on the floor with me. "You're no good. You're no good."

My loving, normally compassionate wife found just the words I needed. They went something like this:

"You're not doing this. Get up and figure it out."

WELCOME TO THE JOURNEY

MAY 31, 2016

WHEN I CLIMB New Mexico's Wheeler Peak (as I have every summer in recent years), I experience two emotional highs. The first comes when I see the mountains; I guess it's the memories of adventures-past and the thrill of once again pitting myself against the peak. The second follows, after the summit, when I'm overcome with a sense of accomplishment, and looking forward to a hot shower, good meal and well-earned rest with hiking buddies.

On this the first official day of retirement, my feelings are more like the first. I'm not overly excited about sleeping in on Mondays (although I can now). I'm more taken with thoughts of a new challenge, a peak to climb if you will, with unfamiliar trails, unknown demands (physical, mental, maybe even spiritual), and, of course, unrealized dreams.

And I have so many—dreams that is. You'll hear about them and you'll experience the ups and downs of retirement —at least the first 60 days or so. Because, through this blog, I intend to take you along.

It'll be therapeutic (I see things more clearly when I write them down), and, besides, my pleasure in hiking is always multiplied by the number of friends who share the journey.

I hope you enjoy.

THE HISTORY OF AMERICAN RETIREMENT IN FOUR SKETCHES

"Life is too long for a single-minded pursuit of safety and material comforts."

— HOWARD AND MARIKA STONE

The Marriage Magnet

IN *THE EVOLUTION OF RETIREMENT*, *1880-1990*, Dora Costa traced the beginning of large-scale retirement in the U.S. to Union Army veterans, who were given pensions by a nation grateful for their sacrifices in the Civil War (Confederate soldiers received no assistance). By 1910, over 90% of these vets were receiving the benefit. And while the annual amount for that pensioner seems low by modern standards ($135 per year), it amounted to over half the annual income of farm workers of the era.[1]

In addition, for the aging (unmarried) vet, there was another, more salient advantage of the program. It attracted young wives who would inherit the benefit at the death of their elderly and, no doubt, smiling spouses. It turned out that way for John Janeway, a Union horse soldier who, in 1927, married Gertrude Grubb, 18, in the middle of a dirt road outside Blaine, Tennessee. Janeway was 81. Three years later, he and his new bride bought a three-room log cabin where he would live until his death in 1937 at age 91.[2]

And the arrangement went well for Gertrude, too, who, 70 years later, told the Associated Press her husband had been the love of her life. When she died in 2003, she still lived in that three-room cabin and still received her veteran's pension (which had escalated to $70 per month). At age 93, Gertrude Janeway was the last surviving widow of a Civil War Union soldier.[3]

The First Social Security Recipient

The first recipient of a monthly Social Security check was 65-year-old Ida May Fuller who, while on another errand, dropped by the Rutland, Vermont office on January 31, 1940 to ask about possible benefits. "It wasn't that I expected anything, mind you, but I knew I'd been paying for something called Social Security and I wanted to ask the people in Rutland about it." Fuller left with Social Security check number 00-000-001 in the amount of $22.54.[4]

Fuller was a perfect candidate for the new benefit. Speaking on August 14, 1935 when he signed the law, President Franklin Roosevelt said this:

"We can never insure one hundred percent of the population against one hundred percent of the hazards and vicissitudes of life, but we have tried to frame a law which will give some measure of protection to the average citizen and to his family against the loss of a job and against poverty-ridden old age."[5]

Known as Aunt Ida to friends and family, Fuller was that average citizen who would need help in old age. She had worked as a teacher and legal secretary in the heart of Vermont's Green Mountains, which would become famous as the birthplace of then future President Calvin Coolidge. Aunt Ida never married and had no children. When she died at age 100, she had been living with a niece in Brattleboro, Vermont. Ida May received $22,888.92 in lifetime Social Security benefits. Shortly before her death, she told a reporter that the payments "come pretty near paying for my expenses."[6]

Living the Dream in Sun City

"We love all the things you can do out here," said Dr. Chester L. Meade in a 1962 piece in *Time*. Meade was referring to the new Dell Webb retirement development in Sun City, Arizona, a place that would set the standard for similar, age-segregated communities to open mostly in the southern states over the next several decades.[7]

Described as a "tanned, lithe, white-haired man," Meade had given up his dental practice of 50 years to move from Mason City, Iowa. "Back there," Meade told the reporter, "you can play golf only a few months of the year. The rest of the time you go to the Elks Club and play two-bit rummy." Of course, there was a reason for the disparity. Mason City's average January high is 24.7 F. The average low is 7.1 F. In Sun City, it's 67 and 41. By February, the high goes to 72.[8]

Meade's wife, Mabel, had her own reasons for the move. "We love children," she said. "But as you get older, you don't care about having a lot of them around. The fact that you can have your own yard and flowers without worrying about children traipsing through is appealing." Mabel also enjoyed the camaraderie: "It's wonderful having everybody on the same level. Here they're not interested in your financial status the way they are in most communities." The Meades weren't alone in their enthusiasm. On opening day January 1, 1960, the developers expected to attract 10,000 visitors. Over 100,000 showed up.[9]

Three years later, the sign welcoming people to the city read "Dell Webb's Sun City, Arizona. Where Active Retirement Originated. Population January 1, 1960: 0. Population January 1, 1963: 7,000. Total Clubs and Organizations: 90. Total States Represented: 50. Motel. Shopping Center. Medical Building. Two Golf Courses."[10]

The Meades would never return to Iowa. Chester lived another 10 years, dying at age 86. Mabel passed in 1989 at 92. They are buried side by side in Sunland Memorial Park, still another Dell Webb amenity in Sun City, Arizona.

Too Young to Retire

"Could we idle away the hours making small talk, puttering around the garden, decorating or redecorating our condo, and waiting for visits from our grandchildren to break the tedium of a life that was without direction or purpose?" asked Marika Stone. The year was 1998, and she and husband Howard were conducting a trial run at retirement, taking time off from successful careers in the Northeast and spending some winter weeks at a second home in Palm Springs, California.[11]

After much reading and reflection, they decided that traditional retirement (i.e. the Sun City experience) was not for them. "The one-size-fits-all formulas that served as retirement planning in their [the Stones' grandparents'] day are inadequate in ours," wrote the couple. "Life is too long for a single-minded pursuit of safety and material comforts."[12]

So the Stones quit their jobs only to begin new ones as a life coach (Howard) and yoga instructor (Marika). Later, they would write a book to chronicle both their journey and the journeys of others opting for a more engaged, post-career experience (the Stones say we need to retire the concept of retirement). The name of their work reflected their passion: *Too Young to Retire: 101 Ways to Start the Rest of Your Life.*

In addition to the book and a website (www. 2young2retire.com) the Stones went on to develop a course that trained others in their vision of an engaged, older society. By 2007, 126 graduates of the program operated in 30 states as well as Canada, Australia and Europe. In 2012, the Stones sold the business to release themselves for more time with family and an active involvement in environmental causes. According to their 2018 Facebook profiles, Howard (now in his 80s) was playing piano in a jazz band, and Marika was still teaching yoga and had taken up the guitar.

IT BEGAN WITH A DRIVE IN THE COUNTRY

JUNE 1, 2016

DID I tell you we're building a house?

So what would make a reserved, conservative couple—one who buys new cars only when the old ones are exhausted and who live in the same house they bought 35 years ago and paid off the mortgage on 10 years ago—what would make such a couple (closing in on their seventh decade) throw caution to the wind and build their dream home?

I'm still not sure. I only know it began with a drive in the country, which led to the discovery of an ideal look (plan), which led to a realignment of investments and budget and then hiring the right builder to make it happen.

And I know that working on the house this spring brought hope to a time that could have focused on loss. I'd look at my students and smile at their futures, then drive to the country and smile at my own.

And I know that the creative process has brought a level of surprise and excitement we have not known since our early days at Hidden Falls Ranch.

I'm new to this retirement business, and it's too soon to say whether building was a good decision. I only know it has filled us with joy. And, for now, that's enough.

2

NOT YOUR GRANDFATHER'S
RETIREMENT

"What if we could have lots of added years but spend them being physically fit, mentally sharp, functionally independent, and financially secure?"

— LAURA CARSTENSEN

I DID—DO something about it, that is. I did what writing teachers do. I wrote. Well, first I researched, then wrote, then researched some more, then wrote some more. You get the idea. It took time—a long time. There were dozens of books and hundreds of articles. I started with the bestsellers, then discovered and read their sources, then returned to less popular books and followed their sources.

What did I learn? I'll spend the rest of this book telling you, but I'll start with this: American retirement is evolving. It is changing because of both a staggering increase in number of retirees and a parallel increase in the length of their life spans.

Actually, sociologists and economic futurists have been

talking about the numbers for some time. In 1999, psychologist/gerontologist Ken Dychtwald authored *Age Power: How the 21ˢᵗ Century Will Be Ruled by the New Old*. In it he wrote,

> During the 20ᵗʰ century, the number of Americans who are 65+ has increased elevenfold, from 3 million to 33 million. According to the U.S. Census Bureau, by 2035 some 70 million people, of whom 60 million will be elder boomers, will be age 65 and older. This is a number more than twice the current population of Canada.[1]

In 2011, the first baby boomers (the mega generation born between 1946 and 1964) turned 65. Since then, they have been joined by 10,000 of their peers every day. According to Pearls and Silver, half of all boomers will live past age 85, which brings up the longevity issue.[2]

A year before Dychtwald's book, Drs. John Rowe and Robert Kahn came out with *Successful Aging*, a work based on the groundbreaking MacArthur Foundation Study, which claimed, at the time, to be the most extensive, comprehensive study on aging in America. Like Dychtwald, Rowe and Kahn wrote about the sheer numbers of the new oldsters. "It is currently estimated that of all the human beings who have ever lived to be sixty-five years or older, half are currently alive."[3]

The doctors said that the increase was due at first to a decrease in infant mortality and death rates in children (mostly because of cures for infectious diseases). This came in the late 19ᵗʰ and first half of the 20ᵗʰ century. A second increase came more recently, during the last several decades, when death rates declined among middle-aged and older Americans. Rowe and Kahn attributed this to "people taking better care of themselves and science and medicine taking better care of people."[4]

But the underlying thesis of the Rowe and Kahn book was not that there were *more* older people, but more *healthy* older people. The MacArthur study found that the idea of older people becoming sicker and more dependent with age was largely a myth. Contrarily, Rowe and Kahn wrote, seniors are "more likely to age well than to become decrepit and dependent." They pointed out, for instance, that only 5.2% of the age group reside in nursing homes. And the new oldsters tended to be free of disabilities. "Of those aged 64 to 74 in 1994, a full 89% reported no disability at all."[5]

It's news like this that caused psychologist Laura Carstensen to write, "What if we could have lots of added years but spend them being physically fit, mentally sharp, functionally independent, and financially secure? At that point, we no longer have a story about old age. We have a story about long life."[6] Cartensen, who is the founding director of the Stanford Center on Longevity, entitled her 2009 book *A Long Bright Future: Happiness, Health, and Financial Security in an Age of Increased Longevity.*

Shockingly, today's boomers will live 30 years longer than their counterparts in the beginning of the 20th century. According to the CDC, in 1900, life expectancy in America was 47.3 years. In 2010, it was 78.7.[7] Even more, if you had lived to age 65 in 2010, you could expect another 19.1 years (taken together, that's 84.1).[8] "Those of us living today have been handed a remarkable gift," wrote Carstensen, "with no strings attached: an extra thirty years of life for the average person."[9]

Moreover, according to Marc Freedman, "All those years that have been added to life spans haven't simply been tacked onto the end. They have been contributed to the middle— mostly to the second half of life where health and capacity after fifty are being dramatically stretched."[10] In *The Big Shift: the New Stage Beyond Midlife*, Freedman called it an "encore stage" and an "encore adulthood."[11] Gail Sheehy (*New Passages*) called it "bonus years" or the "bonus stage."[12] Sara Lawrence-Lightfoot called it the "3rd Chapter."[13] Mary Catherine Bateson (a professor emeritus at George Mason U.) named it "Adulthood II.[14]" She went on to say it was like "composing a further life." Wrote Bateson, "I like to think of men and women as artists of their own lives, working with what comes to hand through accident or talent to compose and re-compose a pattern in time that expresses who they are and what they believe in."[15]

So what's not to like about retirees living longer and healthier than any generation in American history? "Houston, we have a problem." Well, that's almost what Marc Freedman said. In 2011, this social entrepreneur and aging expert said that traditional retirement had become "both unattainable for most individuals, and unsustainable for a society soon to have more people over 60 than under 15."[16]

I'll not write about the unsustainable part. Whole books have been written about the Social Security crisis. Just remember that the program was not meant to sustain an older populace for 30 years. When it was conceived in 1935, life expectancy in the U.S. was 59.9 for men and 63.9 for women.

What hit me was the unattainable part. I thought I was the only one (or one of a minority) who would need to find a way to supplement retirement. But the research was overwhelming. No one (except the writers of those glossy advertisements found in financial magazines) expected us to have the Sun City experience of Charles and Mabel Meade.

Freedman said that the whole idea of a lifestyle of uninterrupted leisure was a recent invention, begun in the 1950s, which through the work of advertisers (not those actually observing life experiences) became the cornerstone of the American Dream. "A leisured retirement became a symbol of a life well lived, and whoever got there first was deemed all the more successful."[17] Pollan wrote that it was an "idea that worked for one generation only, and that was because of a demographic fluke."[18]

Added Pollan, "If someone is rich enough, they'll be able to retire at age 65...and lead the same lifestyle they led when they were working... But for you, for most of my clients, and for subsequent generations of average Americans, the traditional notion of retirement is impossible."[19]

Mitch Anthony (*The New Retirementality*) put it like this: "What we once called retirement—because those who retired stopped working—we now see as a life transition to other work, less work, or very little work."[20] Words like these led me to conclude that if I was hoping for the Sun City style experience of Charles and Mabel Meade, I was going to be disappointed. However, if I could adopt the pioneering spirit of a Howard and Marika Stone (already beginning to resonate with me), I just might find my future liberating, even exciting.

A CHARMED LIFE

JUNE 8, 2016

MOVERS WILL BE HERE today to take our furniture to a storage unit where it will sit until the new place is ready. So tonight Char and I will sleep on a mattress in the living room of an empty house.

We've done this before (if you see a trend here, it seems we seniors have always done something before). In the fall of 1968, we spent our first night together in similar circumstances in a rent house on North 28th Street. Now, the spot is a parking lot for the WTAMU Activity Center.

I wish I could go back in time and visit with the young man in that house. He couldn't believe a gal so beautiful had said "I will" and "I do." I'd tell him that the beauty ran deep and had staying power, and that he was as lucky as he imagined himself.

And I'd say what I will say to myself tonight—that I'm living a charmed life with this lady, and I don't want to waste a moment of it.

3

IF YOU'RE NOT WORRIED YET, YOU SHOULD BE

"Forty-nine percent of middle-class Americans are on track to be living in or near poverty after they quit working."

— TERESA GHILARDUCCI

A CASUAL LOOK at the Web shows that Americans are not overly optimistic about retirement. The following titles, which came up in a Google search for "retirement crisis" during the fall of 2018, make the point:

"What Happens If We All Run Out of Money for Retirement?" (USNews.com)

"SEC Commissioner Warns: The Retirement Crisis Is a Tsunami That Is Rapidly Approaching" (Forbes.com)

"There Is a Retirement Crisis. And Workers Can't Fix It Alone" (Marketwatch.com)

"Many Americans Will Not Be Able to Live Out Their Retirement Dreams" (cnbc.com)

"15 Retirement Statistics That Will Scare the Crap Out of You" (cheatsheet.com)

Why all the negativity? Traditionally, American retirement income has been built on a three-legged stool: Social Security, pensions and savings. Today, each is in trouble.

Financial planners say that retirees need 80% of their pre-retirement earnings to maintain their present lifestyle (70% if one has a paid-off home mortgage);[1] a minority of planners are more pessimistic, predicting the need is more like 110% of previous earnings (I guess all those things on our bucket lists). Yet, for most middle class retirees, Social Security will replace only 40% of income. In 2017, the average monthly payment was $1,583 for men and $1,232 for women, a level barely above the national poverty level ($1,005 for a single and $1,353 for a couple).[2]

Can pensions make up some of the difference? They could if most of us still had them. In the 1960s, 75% of American workers were covered by an employer provided pension, but by 2009, that number was down to 50%. Today, if employers offer a retirement benefit at all, they contribute to a voluntary 401K.[3] About the only present-day retirees with good pensions are public sector employees (federal, state or local workers) who make up just over 15% of the labor force.[4]

So, most are forced to rely on the third leg of the stool, personal savings, to make up the shortfall. But here the news is even more depressing. According to one survey, one-third of baby boomers approaching retirement have less than $25,000 in savings.[5] Another survey said 42% of this group haven't started saving at all.[6]

How much should we have in savings? The experts say eight times our annual pre-retirement income. Using Census Bureau stats for 2014, that would be just short of $600,000 for the average American retiree household.

So, should we delay retirement? Probably, say the experts, if we can. In a 2015 survey, one in 10 Americans said they planned not to retire before 60 but 36% had to do so anyway. Twenty-nine percent retired between 60 and 64; only 9% at 65. One-fourth said they would work until 70, but only 6% of those surveyed did so. The choice was not always up to the worker. Forty percent of respondents were forced to retire earlier than planned, with personal health or health of a family member cited as the reason for more than half of those retirements.[7]

What about part-time employment? According to Teresa Ghilarducci, a finance writer for *The New York Times*, *Money* and *Kiplinger*, "70 isn't the new 50; it's the new 17."[8] That's why you see all those older people taking low-paying jobs at McDonald's and Walmart. It's where the part-time jobs are.

And I've not mentioned healthcare. Medicare is a great thing, but it doesn't pay all the medical bills even for those who have Medicare Advantage or a Medi-gap plan. According to a study conducted by Fidelity Insurance, retirees can expect to pay $285,000 for post-retirement health-care.[9] And that doesn't include the astronomical amount that could be needed for long-term care.

Ghilarducci confirmed my worst fears: "Forty-nine percent of middle-class Americans are on track to be living in or near poverty after they quit working. They'll have a food budget of about $5 a day... If you're not worried," she opined, "you probably don't understand the situation."[10]

No wonder I was on the floor.

But I'm not through. There can be negative psychological

fallout from retirement as well. As it turned out, my mental-emotional collapse was predictable. Writing over 50 years ago, when Dr. Meade was still hitting the fairways at Sun City, Harvard gerontologist Natalie Cabot discovered that retirees suffered a "shocking change in status and identity." We "become a minority almost overnight, and it hits hard, usually within the first three weeks."[11]

Similarly, life-transitions expert William Bridges wrote that every transition begins with an ending. "We have to let go of the old before we can pick up the new." But that's hard, said Bridges, because of fear. The ending "breaks our connection with the setting in which we have come to know ourselves and awakens old memories for hurt and shame." He went on to say we begin to wonder whether the change was good.[12]

Looking back on that Saturday morning, all I could say was "Amen, brother." I certainly had awakened some scary memories, and I was painfully aware that my change may not have been good. I was equally aware there was no going back. My employer would not hire me in a similar position. That's why colleges offer buy-outs; there are already too many full, tenured (read "expensive") professors. And my old house was not going to "unsell" and the new one "unbuild" itself.

As I said, no wonder I was on the floor.

Fortunately, research showed me a way forward, but it wouldn't come through traditional retirement.

ON BUILDING A NEW HOME

JANUARY 10, 2017

DON'T BUILD a new home the same year you retire.

Never.

In 1967, psychiatrists Thomas Holmes and Richard Rahe developed a stress scale to determine how likely people were to become ill because of traumatic life events (for instance, they gave death of a spouse 100 out of a possible 100 stress points; divorce, 73 points; getting married was a 50).

After surveying over 5,000 medical patients, the doctors determined that folks with under 150 points were unlikely to become seriously ill in the next two years; people with 150 to 299 points had a moderate to high chance, and those over 300 had a very high risk of stress-induced illnesses.

So in June (about halfway through our building experience), I scored a 272 on their scale (the points came from events related to either retirement, building a new home or both). I'm convinced I stayed healthy only by the grace of God and a rigorous schedule on the bicycle.

So never, ever build a new home in the same year you retire.

Unless—in tomorrow's blog (page 157), I'll tell you why building that home was the best decision we ever made.

4
_____

IT TAKES A DREAM

"Your life is not about making money—your money is about making a life."

— Mitch Anthony

"I want you to imagine that you are financially secure, that you have enough money to satisfy all of your needs, now and in the future. The question is...how would you live your life?"[1]

George Kinder's question led not only to a clear vision of my dreams, but the realization that there are two competing views of retirement. The first, I'll call the traditional approach, teaches that it's all about money. You sit down with your financial planner who wants to know how much you have and where it is invested. He or she then uses the 80% rule to see how you will need to realign things to achieve the standard of living to which you are accustomed. Oh, a perceptive agent might ask about your want-to's—just in case there is some surplus. But there's a better chance you'll have a shortfall, in which case you will need to scale back your expenses (can you say "downsize"?).

But the question hints at a competing, somewhat recent view I call the dreams-first approach. Howard and Marika Stone are of this ilk. According to the Stones, "contrary to most retirement advice, making the most of the rest of your life will not depend solely on whether or not you have enough money."[2] Another writer, Mitch Anthony (*The New Retirementality*) may have said it best: "Your life is not about making money—your money is about making a life."[3]

Anthony went on to say that many retirees put the "money cart ahead of the life horse."[4] "It's hard to convince someone who doesn't have the money that it really is not about money." Then what was it about? If money is the cart, what is the horse? "It's about doing what you love, doing what you want," said Anthony.[5] "It's about feeling you matter, that you are and will be noticed and appreciated," said another writer (Schlossberg).[6] Still another said I needed to decide who I am and who I want to be (Bateson).[7] The Stones said it would help to create a new mission statement.[8]

George Kinder (*Life Planning for You: How to Design & Deliver the Life of Your Dreams*) seemed to bring it all together. A financial planner (he called himself a "life planner"), Kinder believed that retirement planning begins with one's dreams. He called it "lighting the torch." Before he would ask about money saved for retirement, he wanted to know about his clients' passions and values, what he called their "sacred purposes" or their "call to greatness."[9] On their first visit to his office, Kinder had people (present and future retirees) answer three questions. Paraphrased briefly, they were

1. If you had all the money you wanted, how would you live your life? What would you do and be?

2. If you had only 5-10 years to live—and your finances were the same as now—would you change anything?
3. If your life ended today, what would you wish you had done or become?[10]

Kinder's questions helped me see why I was so frustrated and anxious. I was so focused on money worries I had lost my sense of "sacred purpose." Put simply, I couldn't see the dream for the money. But Kinder's approach was about more than mental tranquility. It wasn't only that thinking about life dreams made one feel better. Kinder said it was about vision, and vision lights the torch. It gives us that fountain of energy we'll need to get off the apartment floor. What about bankers and budgets and such? "With a torch so bright," wrote Kinder, "nothing can stand in the way."[11]

On a side note, the immediate effect of reading Kinder brought me back to the financial planning (i.e., budget making) I had done before hearing from the banker. I discovered that nothing had changed. Yes, the numbers still worked. I could build the house and pay bills and enjoy some non-essentials. It seems that panic clouds things while dreams can bring them back into focus. Put more succinctly, in the traditional view of retirement, money (budgets) determines one's dreams. In the more recent view, dreams determine budgets. When I started with the dream, I "found" the money to support it.

In addition to his questions, Kinder had clients think of (and write down) an "ideal day," "ideal week" and "ideal year." It was a good idea because it made me think how the answers to these questions would look in an actual schedule. Kinder called these "vision exercises."[12] He said he wanted us to discover not only where we are going or what we will do but who we are.

I'll share my answers to Kinder's questions in another chapter, but first I found I had to deal with two things. I had to make peace with my past, and I had to discover my true identity. Neither was easy.

A LITTLE BIT ADVENTURE JUNKIE
JUNE 12, 2016

PART of the famous Alpine loop between Lake City and Silverton, Engineer Pass is one of Colorado's highest and most dangerous mountain passes. At 12,800 feet it is accessible only in a 4-wheel-drive vehicle and then not when snow-packed or extremely wet.

Which it was a few years ago when Charlotte and I tackled it from the difficult west side (narrow and steep with sheer ledges that drop 1,000 feet or more). Didn't know it was that wet (had rained all night), that is, until we were too near the summit to turn back.

We got through with hymns, praise songs (Okay, some mild profanity on my part) and the grace of God.

An hour later, sitting in our favorite soda fountain in Lake City, I actually said it. "Fun, huh?"

Yep, I guess we're a little bit adventure junkies (a little—I won't attempt Engineer again in those conditions). But, as scary and difficult as Jeeping can be, we love it.

I thought about the Colorado experience yesterday when we finally nailed down a destination for the first segment of our homeless adventure between the old and new house. With the help of generous (and mildly insane) friends and family, we have places to stay for most of the time.

And I'm guessing that this pilgrimage might foreshadow things to come in the greater retirement journey.

If so, it'll be okay—because we're a little bit adventure junkies. A little bit.

5

MAKING PEACE WITH THE PAST

"Your attitudes toward events are sometimes more
important than the events themselves."

— PHILIP ZIMBARDO

SO KINDER WANTED me to articulate my dreams, to imagine a
future, but according to Stanford psychologists Philip
Zimbardo and John Boyd (*The Time Paradox: The New
Psychology of Time That Will Change Your Life*), optimistically
imagining the future is impossible if one is stuck in his past.[1]

For instance, if you are what they called a "past negative"
(focus on things that went wrong in your past, usually with
regret and guilt),[2] you will have a hard time being positive
and hopeful about the future. You can become what they
called a "fatalistic present,"[3] one who doesn't believe there is
anything one can do to make a better future and, thus, makes
arbitrary and unhelpful life choices (I wonder how many of
those who have saved nothing for retirement are "fatalistic
presents"). Or one can become overly occupied with the

future, living a present filled with stress and anxiety and almost no relaxation or play.

I identified with the second of these. For most of my life, I've struggled with anxiety, and, I guess, I've always known it was rooted in the past. For while I have many pleasant memories of childhood, there are bad ones too, most of which were the result of my dad's alcoholism (he wasn't abusive, just sometimes impaired and unable to provide as a husband and father should). The immediate results for his youngest boy centered around speech problems (I was a chronic stutterer and had trouble shaping some sounds). This got better with time, but new problems (read "failures") took its place. Anyway, as years went by, and when I felt stress, I tended to slip into anxiety and preoccupation with those past negatives. I said my words on the apartment floor—"I'm no good; I'm no good"—sounded familiar. They were.

But there is good news. "The past matters," wrote Zimbardo and Boyd, "but not as much as we think. Your attitudes toward events are sometimes more important than the events themselves."[4] The doctors cited a book by Tim Wilson called *Redirect: Changing the Stories We Live By*, where the author's main idea is that we can "edit" and "reshape" our past narratives in a way that will lead to meaning, hope, purpose and optimism.[5]

Wilson had studied Critical Incident Stress Debriefing (CISD), which was once the strategy most used for victims of trauma and grief. The premise of CISD is that when people have experienced a traumatic event, they should air their feelings as soon as possible, so that they don't bottle up these emotions and develop post-traumatic stress disorder (PTSD). Wilson said it was the method of choice for the 9,000 counselors who rushed to New York City after 9/11.[6]

But, according to Wilson, it didn't work. Researchers

"found something unexpected: not only is CISD ineffective, it may *cause* psychological problems." It turns out that making people undergo CISD right after a trauma impedes the natural healing process and might even "freeze" memories of the event.[7]

Wilson discovered that more significant than the traumatic event itself is the interpretation we put on it. "In short, the way in which we interpret the world is extremely important."[8] The doctor advocated "story editing, which is a set of techniques designed to redirect people's narratives about themselves and the social world in a way that leads to lasting changes in behavior." According to Wilson, "Small edits can lead to lasting change."[9] He wanted us to "shape" our narratives, keeping in mind the perspectives of meaning, hope and purpose. He went on to recommend that we shape past narratives with a healthy dose of optimism. "Optimistic people cope better with adversity."[10]

And optimistic people seem to create better dreams for retirement. Before I could do well answering Kinder's three questions, I needed to take Zimbardo's advice and create a "positive reconstruction" of my past. "You cannot change the past," wrote Zimbardo, "but you can change your attitudes toward it."[11] So the Stanford psychologist had readers do three things: one, list significant negative events that have occurred in their lives; two, list positive messages that can be taken from these events; and, three, tell how these lessons can improve their future.[12]

Well, I tried it, first with my speech issues (all improved dramatically over time, and now I speak for a living), and, then, with adulthood traumas (I had failed at both a job and a career). The exercises were so helpful I decided to go a step further. In the Old Testament Book of Nehemiah (chapters 8 and 9), there is a brief summary of Israel's deliverance over several centuries. Each line begins with a statement of the predicament and ends with a declaration of God's faithful rescue. I thought it would be helpful to write a similar history.

With a single sentence for each, I listed all the memorable traumas of my life (about 40) and followed with an equally brief statement of how (and to what extent) I was set free. For instance, as a child I had many worries—that my parents would die, that I would die, that my speech issues would get worse (I know, I was a morbid thinking kid). Anyway, none of the fears came true. None. I did the same with adult traumas. The lost career ended with a new one, the happiest and most productive to date. Even the events that didn't end well —my sister's early death—had some redeeming element— her legacy which lives on in her children or my expectation of meeting her in Heaven.

With newly found optimism, I was ready to answer Kinder's questions. Almost. The research was pointing me to another prerequisite for discovering one's dreams. I needed to deal with identity.

THE BOY WHO WAS I

AUGUST 8, 2016

SAW OLD FRIENDS this week who made me think of him: the boy who was I.

He was an active kid—liked to water ski and snow ski, to ride his bike and his horse, to play football in the fall and baseball in the summer.

The boy who was I craved adventure, especially the outdoor variety: campouts at Palo Duro with his scouting buddies or a long hike along the railroad tracks south of town. Trains and tracks fascinated him, as did train whistles, heard early in the morning when it was still dark. Whistles seemed to call the boy to places and purposes far off—exotic places, beyond his imagination.

Guess that's why the boy was such a dreamer. Guess that's why he still is. William Wordsworth got it right: "The child is father of the man."

6

WHO AM I

"The child is father of the man."

— WILLIAM WORDSWORTH

WHO AM I? Who are you? Well, I'll tell you who we are not.

We are not our former job titles.

We are not our bank balances.

We are not our stage in life (adolescent or retiree).

These lies need to be unmasked for sometimes we must know who we are *not* before we can know who we *are*.[1] And we must know who we are because identity precedes dreams. You dream what you dream because you are who you are. Discover your identity (or identities) and you'll discover your dreams.

How do you discover your identity? The question should be *where* do you discover your identity? And the answer is in your past. Alexander de Tocqueville said, "the entire man is to be seen in the cradle of a child." Poet William Wordsworth wrote, "The child is father of the man." According to sociologist Sara Lawrence-Lightfoot, "Almost every one of the women and men I interviewed found it necessary to begin their stories of Third Chapter learning with flashbacks to their childhoods."[2] Third Chapter is what Lightfoot called the traditional retirement years, and like many other writers on the subject, she said our past holds keys to our future.

Similarly, Marika and Howard Stone said we need to revisit childhood dreams.[3] Dr. Schlossberg (*Revitalizing Retirement: Reshaping Your Identity, Relationships, and Purpose*) said we should construct a personal narrative of the past.[4] Mary Catherine Bateson (*Composing a Further Life*) put it succinctly: "Am I still the person I have spent a lifetime becoming, and do I still want to be that person?"[5]

It was another of those questions that required pen and paper. I divided my life into multi-year segments, starting at birth and ending with my last job before retiring. For each period, I wanted to know what I loved doing and what I was good at doing (they might not be the same). Then, I looked for loves and abilities that showed up in multiple segments. These, I decided, must get in my dreams. Yes, I still wanted to be the person I had spent a lifetime becoming.

In doing this exercise, I was dealing with what Zimbardo called "past positives." It was a more pleasant experience than listing past traumas, but just as necessary. Not only did it foster optimism, but it was insightful. I learned who I was and, thus, who I wanted to be in the future. The "where's" and "what's" of my dream would focus on this. By the way, remember Harvard gerontologist Natalie Cabot? She's the one who said our initial retirement crisis is one of lost identity. Almost overnight we become a disempowered minority. Well, life reviews tell a different story. It seems our identities follow us through life. So when I left Amarillo College, none of these had left me.

Who am I? Following is what I learned from interviews with earlier versions of me (I hope they will motivate you to have similar chats with your former selves). The eight-year-old Mike wanted to talk mostly about his horse, a Paint mare named Sue, which he did in rushed sentences punctuated with the delayed starts of a stutterer. It didn't seem to bother this kid, nor did his pronunciation issues—w's for l's and r's —which made him sound like a boyish Elmer Fudd. The eight-year-old loved to ride bareback through endless prairie and endless summer days. He enjoyed water skiing, swimming, Little League baseball, stream fishing for Rainbow Trout, hanging out with buddies (anywhere, anytime) and some attempts at entrepreneurship—most notably a lemonade stand.

The 12-year-old me was more sullen and reserved, a condition brought on by his dad's worsening alcoholism. But he still had a love for the outdoors, on display with his energetic participation in Boy Scouts. His yearly highlight was Troop 66's trip to the Pecos Wilderness near Santa Fe where he would hike, fish and race homemade, log rafts on Lake Stewart.

My 17-year-old self had found his life passion and purpose (and his future bride) at Hidden Falls Ranch, a Christian youth camp on the rim of Palo Duro Canyon. My interview with him revealed a young man beginning to take an interest in causes and people other than himself. He also was becoming a leader, first as the head wrangler in the horseback riding program, then as director of the counselor in training course and, finally, as program director in charge of all activities. For the first time in his life, he began to find his smile in the smiles of others.

Talking to the 27-year-old me, I was addressing the youngest executive director in the history of Hidden Falls, too young as it seems to this 70-year-old. The job was bigger than he, and he would leave it after only four years. But my job as an interviewer was not to evaluate weakness but abilities and loves, and this young man had become an administrator, good at recruiting and motivating a team, both things he seemed to enjoy.

In the next four decades, I moved from leading faith-based organizations to teaching English on a college campus. The me of this era enjoyed reading and researching. He wrote newspaper columns and a few books. He still liked adventures and enjoyed taking others along. Mostly, he liked to help the underachiever and the hopeless. His greatest joy was making their dreams come true.

When I first wrote these paragraphs, I was embarrassed by how self-flattering and possibly untrue they were (untrue because they were incomplete). But Zimbardo had asked for past positives. My past negatives (read failures) would have made for longer and more interesting stories, but dreams are built on the ideal, the best of what you have been, what you can be, and, hopefully, what you will be.

So putting these all together, I found I am a builder/creator (organizations, books, brick and mortar), adventurer/facilitator (everything from horses to bicycles to cruise ships and I'm happiest if I recruit fellow travelers), teacher/communicator (I like to inform, entertain and inspire if I can) and provider/dream-maker (I like giving both material and nonmaterial help to family, friends and good causes, and nothing has made me happier than helping others see their dreams come true).

Christian theologian and cultural critic Os Guinness would say these are my callings (*The Call*, 2003).[6] Like eye color or stature, they are gifts from God (given at birth, or rebirth, or both), which I had no part in choosing and for which I can take no credit. "What do you have that you did not receive?" asked the Apostle Paul (I Corinthians 4:7). So I did not "create" a calling. I recognized it. From a theological point of view, I did not "find" my calling. Guinness pointed out that the Bible emphasizes God's seeking, not ours.[7] He seeks us, not we Him. I didn't find Him; He found me. He wasn't lost; I was.

Similarly, we don't "find" our calling(s), it (they) find us. Remember the Hans Christian Andersen fairy tale? The ugly duckling wasn't good at being a duck because he wasn't one. He had just ended up in the wrong nest where others told him he was a duck and an ugly one to boot. How did he discover he was really a swan? His calling found him. He saw beautiful swans flying overhead and something stirred in his spirit. Swimming towards swans (his true identity), he looked in the water and discovered in the reflection that he was one.

That's why the experts have us study our histories. We're looking for identities, true reflections of ourselves. And we're noting those stirrings in our spirit—feelings that overwhelmed us when... When what? The answer to that question is the answer to the first one: who am I?

There is one more principle on which the Bible and retirement literature agreed. Our callings exist for more than our own happiness. Guinness said they are "ours for others."[8] and, in pleasing others, we find ourselves pleased, too. Wrote Guinness, "somehow we humans are never happier than when we are expressing the deepest gifts that are truly us."[9]

Now, I was ready to answer Kinder's questions. What would I do if money were no object? How would I spend my days if I knew they were limited? What would I regret not doing if I joined Jesus in Heaven tonight? My interviews told me the answers are revealed by other questions: What do I want to build or create (keeping in mind what it would do for others)? Where would I like to take adventures and with whom? What do I want to teach and where? What subjects would be most likely to inspire and give hope? For whom do I wish to provide and how? How can I help others dreams come true?

KEEPING IT REAL

AUGUST 7, 2016

I'VE ALWAYS TRIED to be honest with readers. Nonfiction guru Lee Gutkind calls it "keeping it real."

So here goes: when I wrote of identities yesterday, I told only half the truth. What I said is that, when we retire, we don't suddenly lose the gifts that made us good at what we did. What I didn't say is that we often do lose the acknowledgement of those abilities.

When I stopped being a camp director, I can't remember ever being asked for advice by new directors. For the record, I didn't ask either (maybe it's because we think we know what our predecessor will say).

Same happened when I left the church. While still a pastor, folks asked how I came up with relevant and moving sermons. And I had plenty of opportunities to deliver them. Not afterwards.

And I'm expecting the same with teaching. I'm not going to get requests from new teachers wanting to know how I motivated students (again, I didn't ask my predecessor either, something I now regret).

So if you live with a retired person who is struggling with lost identity, know that the pain comes not because he or she is unnoticed but unused.

Now, I've come to the point in my blog where I offer hope (a thought to help us deal with unpleasant realities). And I'll do that—tomorrow. For now, and in honor of those who struggle with identity lost, I'll let the pain linger, which it often does for too many retirees.

7

DREAMERS OF THE DAY

"Dreamers of the day are dangerous men, for they may act
their dreams with open eyes, to make it possible."

— T. E. LAWRENCE (LAWRENCE OF ARABIA)

ACCORDING to Richard Leider and Alan Webber (*Life Reimagined: Discovering Your New Life Possibilities*), fear is the major
hindrance to living our retirement dreams. "In the process of
reimagining your life, fear is the enemy."[1] Fear of what? The
authors mentioned fear of the past or the future, of losing
what we've gained or failing to gain new things, of failing in
general or failing to try. The list, they said, is endless. What
will help? It seems taking action will. "Fear is the enemy of
action," they wrote. "Action is the enemy of fear."[2] T. E.
Lawrence (you know him as Lawrence of Arabia) had a
similar thought:

> All men dream: but not equally. Those who
> dream by night in the dusty recesses of their

minds wake in the day to find it was vanity:
but the dreamers of the day are dangerous
men, for they may *act* their dreams with
open eyes, to make it possible.[3]

I agree with Howard and Marika Stone. We need to retire
the concept of retirement.[4] Retirement suggests withdrawal
from most of what's important in life. As children, we were
sent outside to play so we wouldn't be in the way. As retirees,
we are sent outside (i.e. dismissed from meaningful work and
activities) for much the same reason. There's no room in
modern retirement for dangerous men and women, folks
with their eyes wide open in pursuit of dreams that matter
not only to the dreamer but to society as a whole.

There came a point in my journey when it was time to act.
I had recognized my callings and articulated some dreams.
Now it was time to make phone calls: to a banker, a lawyer, a
Real Estate agent, a builder and others.

In *The Call*, Os Guinness highlighted Lawrence's vision
and imagination. The imagination part stuck with me since
the retirement experts cite it often. In *Revitalizing Retirement*,
Dr. Nancy Schlossberg wanted me to imagine the specifics of
my dreams: "What is the scenario you would like to see?
Imagine writing a play about yourself in the future. Let your
imagination soar; later, you can scale down to some realistic
goals."[5] I didn't write a play, but I did visualize walking over
my property and pointing out, to a future visitor, features I
intended to build. I also envisioned hanging out with grandkids and friends in spaces Charlotte and I had created.

Similarly, George Kinder had recommended imagining an
ideal year and day.[6] I took time to visualize an hour-by-hour
day filled with the kind of activities I intended to pursue.
Ditto for a yearly calendar, except I went month by month

and listed the events I wanted to include in my first year after Amarillo College. When we planned our house, Charlotte and I were helped by pictures from the Web—house designs, colors, landscapes, visuals of certain looks we wanted both inside and out. Planning was part of the joy of building, and I expect it will be the same with other dreams.

But action on my dreams took courage—at times, more than I could find in myself (the subject of another chapter). For now, if you are struggling similarly, chances are the biggest fear is financial. So before I start writing about money, maybe it will help to realize what I did—that you have more assets than you think you have, that you can get by on less than you think you can, and, with the new gig economy, that you can supplement revenues more than you dreamed possible.

TOO MUCH A DREAMER

JUNE 6, 2016

I FELT ALONE, anxious and a little hopeful. It was 1995, and I was preparing for a new career by attending grad school at Texas Tech. I can still remember my first walk across campus.

Did I belong there? Could I succeed as a Ph.D. student? Or was I making a horrible mistake? Maybe I was too much of a dreamer.

I remember because I experienced the same thoughts today. I'm walking in unfamiliar territory, and the culture tells me that senior citizens are, well, senior citizens—nice folks, but not particularly strong or intelligent or successful.

Maybe we can succeed (sort of) on a golf course, but these years are not the time to start a new business or invent a new phone app, or write a new book or (you get the drift).

Maybe I'm too much of a dreamer.

8

TAKING INVENTORY

"It's important to see your 'human capital' as part of your
investments and assets."

— GEORGE KINDER

KINDER WAS RIGHT. Starting with dreams added passion and
energy, even to boring things like making a budget. In the
traditional, money-first way of approaching it, I would start
with my assets, then decide how to allocate them so as to
cover all the bases (basic needs with a few luxuries thrown
in). My budget would look much like the pre-retirement
version, only tighter. I wouldn't have as much cash flow.

But Kinder's dream-first model changed the paradigm.
Finances didn't direct dreams; dreams directed finances. The
question became "how do I use these resources to get to my
goals?" Not only was I more motivated; the approach was
more practical. I knew exactly where I wanted my funds
to go.

So I started with a list of monetary resources, or what my

banker called a "confidential financial statement." I listed assets (like Real Estate, automobiles, savings, Social Security, Texas teacher retirement) and then liabilities (debts). According to the banker, the difference between the two is my net worth. Net worth is what I would have to work with to achieve my dreams.

Almost. In the new paradigm, money is not *first* and it is not *all*. Kinder spoke of human capital—things like education, skills, experience in management, computer skills and social networking savvy.[1] His list got me thinking. Aren't my contacts and networks also assets that can create positive cash flow? And what about assets of the spirit—things like optimism, creativity, willingness to learn new things and to take some risk?

On Charlotte's ledger, I added compassion and sensitivity to the needs of others (they may not increase cash flow, but they would certainly add to life satisfaction). Also, I included business opportunities—things unique to my time and place that could lead to new products and services—with more baby boomers traveling, could I transform some rental units to Airbnb properties?

CATCHING A THUNDERSTORM

JULY 25, 2016

CHASED A THUNDERSTORM YESTERDAY.

If you don't live in our part of Texas, you might not know we've had multiple triple-digit days with no relief in sight.

So about 1:00 p.m., Charlotte and I were walking out of a restaurant when we noticed a nice thunderhead in the east.

"Too bad," said my wife (our storms come from the west).

"Let's catch it," said I.

We did—on FM 1151 just west of Claude.

For a moment, we wondered if it had been a good idea—lots of thunder, lightning, high winds and sheets of rain so heavy visibility was reduced to maybe 100 feet. Water was starting to pool on the road, and I felt we could hydroplane any minute.

We looked at each other.

And giggled.

9

BUDGETING 101

"One of the biggest money mistakes people make is to underestimate their spending."

— TERESA GHILARDUCCI

CHRIS HOGAN SAID I should start my budget with income.[1] This would show things listed under assets, which can be monetized. One can withdraw monthly from a 401K. Investment property will generate rental income. However, for most retirees, monthly income will come primarily from Social Security, a pension program, part-time work, or a combination of all three. In my first budget, I didn't worry whether the income would match expenses. I just needed to know where I was starting; then I could think about lowering expenses and raising income.

But before I start on the budgeting process, I need to say— and this is urgent—hang on to the thought of your dreams. This budgeting business is pretty dry stuff, but it's not so bad when you stop and remember the purpose. I would find a picture (or pictures) that look like where you are headed and keep them by your side.

Teresa Ghilarducci (whose little book *How to Retire with Enough Money* is my favorite on financial matters) said to begin budgeting by keeping track of expenses for several months. This way I wouldn't fool myself into thinking I was spending less than I really did. Ghilarducci seemed to think most people underestimate expenses[2] (had she been looking over my shoulder?). And going back several months would make me budget for periodic expenses (like going to the dentist or paying automobile taxes).

Ghilarducci then suggested separating needs from wants. Julie Jason (*The AARP Survival Guide*) called them "musts" and "wants."[3] Mitch Anthony (*The New Retirementality*) divided expenses five ways: survival (have to have), safety (insurance, emergency fund), freedom (travel, relaxation), gifts (to people or causes) and dream expenses (one's bucket list).[4] Miriam Goodman (*Reinventing Retirement*) called the dream category an "impulse fund" (splurging for a weekend retreat or a generous gift to a friend).[5]

Dave Ramsey said that however I divided it, I needed to make sure I had a category for every dollar I received in income. This is called zero-sum budgeting. The revenue and expenses add up to zero. According to Ramsey, people who use the zero-sum approach pay off 19% more debt and save 18% more money—just from having a plan.[6] His words reminded me that even though I wouldn't be saving as much, I still needed to save some in post-retirement. If nothing else, if we live as long as the charts say, it would keep us up with inflation (half of baby boomers are supposed to live until 85).

As I write these words, it's been nearly three years since I made that first, postretirement, handwritten budget. Looking at it today, some categories make me smile. I've consistently come in about $150 below what I anticipated for utilities and $300 less than what I budgeted for monthly house payments (including taxes and insurance). On the other hand, income has been exactly as planned, except for revenue producers I added later (see chapter eleven). However, I left off a big expense category—monthly withholding for federal income tax. I was used to the automatic deductions in my college paycheck, but my new revenue streams don't do that. So I'm optimistic about the process—budgets do work—but I'll need to continue making adjustments.

HORNY TOADS

JULY 6, 2016

Saw several horny toads on my bike ride today. Actually, they're not toads but lizards, the Texas Horned Lizard to be exact. We call them "horny" not because of sexual predilection but because that's what everyone else calls them in this part of Texas.

"Seen any horny toads lately?"

On the elementary school playground, my friend Jack hypnotized horny toads. He'd turn them over and rub their tummies, and they'd go all limp. Looked hypnotized to me, but Jack never tested to be sure. He could have.

"When you wake," (speaking to the lizard with the look of Bela Lugosi as Dracula) "you'll be a vicious German Shepherd, and Mike is threatening your master."

At summer camp, we raced horny toads. We would capture likely speedsters, place them alongside those of fellow counselors and await the starter's whistle. The idea was to coax your entry (by stepping close behind, shouting and herding him or her) to the finish line.

We raced frogs and long-tailed lizards (maybe the six-lined racerunner), too. Frogs were erratic, which usually got them squished by overeager handlers. Long-tailed lizards were too fast. Even if you could keep one on a straight line, you were unlikely to catch it again, which you had to do to win the race.

What does this have to do with retirement? Maybe this: I haven't thought of racing horny toads since I was a boy, and, just maybe, my life has room for him again (i.e. the boy not the toad).

10

SUBTRACT BEFORE YOU ADD

"You can live far more comfortably with less than you thought possible."

— HOWARD STONE

MITCH ANTHONY CALLED it "negotiating with your needs."[1] Obviously, since I was going from a mortgage-free existing house to a financed new one, and since my pension from the State of Texas didn't match the monthly income I had received from teaching, I needed to do some negotiating on the needs side.

Again, it's important to the dreams-first approach to keep in mind your purpose. Everything you are able to subtract from your budget makes room for a bit more of your dream. You're not denying the best pleasures; you're expanding them.

Howard Stone was reassuring: "Here is a little secret from the Voluntary Simplicity movement the retirement industry would just as soon you don't find out: You can live far more comfortably with less than you thought possible."[2] So how does one start subtracting? Most retirement authors want us to begin by eliminating debt, including a mortgage on one's home. Kinder is an exception. On the page immediately following one where he said to "simplify life, save money and invest," he wrote "leverage your home." Like others who have made money in Real Estate, Kinder's idea was that the return on investment is greater when borrowing than when owning outright.[3]

Of course, the problem with this was cash flow. If I was going from no payment to a substantial one, I would need to find new money for that. And I did. We renegotiated a loan on investment property that freed up enough monthly funds to cover the new house payment plus insurance and taxes. I knew Dave Ramsey would not be happy with me, but my monthly debt to income ratio was virtually the same as before.

I did realize I was an outlier. Most retirement experts (Ghilarducci is an example) recommended downsizing—finding a smaller home or "finding a nice home in a modest neighborhood."[4] Whatever one decides, homes are a big part of most retirees' assets, and a change here can free up capital or reduce monthly expenditures dramatically. If one's dream is to travel extensively, selling a home and renting might be a good way to invest wisely and finance the trips.

Practically all the experts recommended eliminating credit card debt, which we had done some time ago. A few (Stone, Ramsey, Hogan) said to stop using cards completely, which we didn't. I knew Ramsey presented stats to show people spend more if they use credit, but if we were keeping a budget and paying the card balance every month with no fee,

I didn't see a problem. Besides, let's face it; it's more convenient.

Ghilarducci said to get rid of all debt, including home mortgages. I didn't take her advice on the house, but did pay off the only non-Real Estate loan we had—on a vehicle. Speaking of vehicles, Kinder and Ghilarducci recommended driving used cars. Ghilarducci said that new cars lose 20% when they leave the lot.[5] And, evidently, we shouldn't be scared by high mileage. My friend Stuart is in charge of a fleet of vehicles operated by a regional health care provider, vehicles used to get people and materials to various locations. He told me his company never buys a used ambulance. But the great majority of other vehicles are bought with high mileage —over 100K on average. And some of these are still running well after 300K. Stuart said the trick is to buy vehicles known for longevity and to provide consistent maintenance, especially oil changes.

I've just scratched the surface of what I was reading. One can find a number of books and authors giving practical advice for cutting expenses. Kinder recommended renting (as opposed to going to) movies, comparing insurance policies, raising deductibles on most of those policies (this strategy saved us a lot), buying clothes at resale shops (Charlotte loved that one) and finding inexpensive leisure like biking or hiking (I liked this one).[6] Ghilarducci recommended buying term rather than whole life insurance, avoiding protection plans on appliances (usually the warranty is adequate) and, when eating out, forgoing beverages and dessert. I decided I could take her advice on the beverage.[7]

In addition, several of my regular monthly expenses were automatically reduced or eliminated by retirement. I would no longer have teacher retirement and 401K contributions withheld from my check. I would have less fuel expense, less clothing expense and, because of a lower income, less income tax. Total savings from all the above was substantial, but I had a lot of dreams. I still wanted more income.

BANANA PUDDING
AUGUST 3, 2016

HAD A SALAD FOR LUNCH TODAY.

In case you're thinking I'm a healthy eater, you should know I had banana pudding for supper last night.

No, not for dessert.

I said I had banana pudding *for supper* last night.

And before you start judging me, you should know banana pudding has milk and eggs and bananas and vanilla wafers.

Just for the record, that's four of the five basic food groups.

Just sayin'.

11

COON SKIN CAPS AND HULA-HOOPS

"People will pay a lot of money to fulfill their dreams."

— MARY FURLONG

WHAT IF YOU could add more dollars to fund more dreams? Who wouldn't like that? Well, the literature says my generation has unparalleled opportunity to do just that.

"So many people who are at what in the past would be retirement age, recognize that they're nowhere near done, and at the same time that they can't afford to be done." The words, which appeared in a 2015 article in *Forbes*,[1] came from Marc Freedman, a renowned social entrepreneur and founder/CEO of Encore.org. I was already familiar with Freedman. For the last 20 years, I had been writing about baby boomers in midlife, and Marc Freedman was a significant voice of change for the way we do late-in-life careers. His 2007 book, *Encore: Finding Work That Matters in the Second Half of Life*, told the stories of successful men and women who left primary, well-paying careers to work for non-profit, philanthropic organizations where they would, among other things, mentor young leaders. Freedman's organization helped match these "retirees" with the civic-minded groups. The work was sometimes part-time, sometimes full, sometimes paid, and sometimes voluntary. That would work for me if I wanted another cause to champion, but my cup was already full. What I needed was something short on hours and long on income. Yeah, right. Only in my dreams? Well, yes, I did want a job(s) that would finance—without getting in the way of—my dreams.

It turned out the experts were all over this one. Those who had studied both aging and the baby boom generation knew we boomers were headed for a financial crisis and would need extra to make retirement work. Thus, in 2013, AARP published a list of best employers of people over 50.[2] Also, many of the books I had read had sections on good, part-time jobs for retirees. The best was a chapter in *Too Young to Retire*. It's called "101 Opportunities for the Open Minded."[3] Following are some of their suggestions: antique restorer, bed and breakfast host, cake decorator, clown (hopefully, not a scary one), cruise ship lecturer, dog walker, massage therapist and tutor (buy the Stones' book and read the whole list; it's worth the price).

Similarly, Mark Miller (*The Hard Times Guide to Retirement Security*) wrote that Americans ages 55 to 65 were starting businesses at the highest rate of any age group: "28 percent higher than the average of all adults."[4] The best book I found on this subject was *The Retirement Rescue Plan* by Melissa Phipps, whose subtitle was "Retirement Planning Solutions for the Millions of Americans Who HAVEN'T SAVED ENOUGH" (capital letters are hers). In a chapter called "New Income Streams," Phipps detailed several opportunities for retiree businesses, including what she called the "sharing economy job." "If you are looking for short-term jobs or 'gigs,' the sharing economy helps connect you to people who need your services."[5]

Examples of these are peer-to-peer property rentals like Airbnb and Homeaway (you can rent a single room or your whole house, for one day or several months), and peer-to-peer ride sharing businesses like Uber and Lyft ("half of Uber's drivers are older than 40"[6]). Phipps said that, through a company called RelayRides, one could even "rent out a second car to people looking for a discount rental."[7] The beauty of these businesses is that they are Internet based where the company takes care of most of the hard stuff (applications and screening of customers, marketing, payment). So I could do almost everything with a good smart phone.

It's hard to overstate what the idea of starting new businesses meant to me. From lemonade stands as a child, to lawn and firewood selling ventures as a teen, I had enjoyed the challenge of entrepreneurship. I guess it spoke to the adventurer and builder in me. With our rental properties, Charlotte and I already had one small business, and as I write these words, I'm hard at work on two other projects, activities exciting as any class I have taught.

In 1988, I wrote about the economic impact made by my generation, the 80 million American baby boomers born between 1946 and 1964 (*Baby Boom Believers*, Tyndale House). I mentioned both coonskin caps and hula-hoops:

> In 1955 Fes Parker first donned the buckskins of Davy Crockett, and the wholesale price of raccoon skins went from $.26 to $8.00 a pound. Before it ended, the Crockett craze gave us over three thousand varieties of Davy's paraphernalia, everything from sweatshirts to tooth-

brushes... In 1958 Wham-O Corporation invented the hula-hoop, and by year's end 20,000 per day were being produced.[8]

The good news is that the economic power of the baby boom is now stronger than ever. Dr. Mary Furlong wrote of it in her 2007 book *Turning Silver into Gold: How to Profit in the new Boomer Marketplace.* The title gives it away. Considered a leading expert on the boomer and longevity market, Furlong told business leaders how to create products and services to be consumed by a generation that in 2007 earned two trillion dollars a year and owned more than 77% of all financial assets."[9]

Furlong got me thinking about future business ventures. It seems that pursuing dreams is not only something that can make us happy; if we help others do the same, it might make us wealthy. Wrote Furlong, "People will pay a lot of money to fulfill their dreams."[10]

50 YEARS OF STUFF

JUNE 7, 2016

I'T's a Claude High School letter jacket worn by my wife in 1966 when the Lady Mustangs were Bi-District Champs. And it's the reason we're arguing.

She wants to throw it away. "I don't need it, and our kids won't want it," she says.

"But it's history," I say. "One day, a little girl will look at it and know her great-great grandmother was good at basketball."

"I wasn't that good," she says, "and we don't have room in the new house."

"Okay," says I. "So what about these?" I'm holding a pair of knickers I wore on the slopes of Red River in 1967.

"You haven't fit in those since we married," she says.

"But it's history. One day a little boy will know his great-great grandfather..."

And so it goes—as my minimalist wife and her packrat husband sort through nearly 50 years of stuff.

This is going to take a while.

12

INVESTING FOR DUMMIES

"How you invest *during* retirement is as critical as how you invest in preparing for retirement."

— DANIEL R. SOLIN

I FEEL my eyes beginning to glass over as I write these words, which was my response when first reading the investment sections of most retirement books. I titled this chapter "Investing for Dummies" because, in the words of Curly of Three Stooges fame, "I resemble that remark." I have never been an astute student of Wall Street.

But since I had some funds in a 401K, and because my dreams relied on managing this asset well, I decided I had better know the difference between a stock and a bond. And there were plenty of people wanting to tell me; that is, a large portion of the authors I read discussed investments.

In the end, I chose four to be my guides. Julie Jason was an investment advisor living in Stanford, Connecticut and author of *The AARP Survival Guide*.[1] Dan Solin was a financial advice columnist for the *Huffington Post* and author of *The Smartest Retirement Book You'll Ever Read*.[2] Teresa Ghilarducci wrote for the *New York Times* and *Money* and had written *How to Retire with Enough Money*.[3]

My fourth expert—I'll call him Steve the Economics Prof —was not an author but a friend and colleague.[4] I had consulted Steve on several money matters through the years and thought it good to include someone who didn't make his living selling investments but buying them.

And Steve has been a lifelong investor. He started a savings account when still in elementary school. By high school, he was reading *The Wall Street Journal* and had his own Merrill Lynch account. I wondered how such frugality began at such an early age. He told me his maternal grand-parents, who had lived through the depression, encouraged their grandkids to save. Besides," he told me, "I guess I'm just wired that way." I think my friend was being humble (and kind to those of us who don't share his experience). His words made me wish I had listened more as a child, and I made a note to offer similar advice to my grands.

What do the experts say about investing? Ghilarducci said that most investors spread their holdings between stocks and bonds.[5] Stocks are like part-ownerships in companies. Your amount of shares tells you how much you own. Bonds are like loans made to companies (or cities or even the govern-ment). Usually, younger investors are encouraged to purchase stocks. They have a higher risk of losing value in the short run (if you should need to sell), but stocks also have a history of making money in the long run (about 10% a year according to Hogan[6]). By the way, Steve said 10% is a best case scenario. Because of some technical changes (had to do with FED policy over the last several years), Steve thinks the average is now closer to 6%.

Bonds, on the other hand, are less risky. Solin said bonds would generate a steady income in retirement while protecting my principal[7] (the money I had first put in). At my age, both Solin and Ghilarducci recommended a portfolio heavier on bonds than stocks. However, I would still need stocks because I needed some growth just to keep up with inflation. So that's what I did. I changed from a portfolio heavy on stocks to one of mostly bonds. Steve said *less risk* does not mean *no risk*. When interest rates go up, bond values go down. I would need professional advice on when to buy and sell.

My experts advocated diversified, indexed funds as opposed to actively managed funds (this applied to both stocks and bonds). Indexed means the fund is tied (indexed) to a group of stocks, say the Dow Jones Industrial Average. Thus, the fund will perform over time very close to the same as the Dow (about 10% a year on my money). By contrast, actively managed funds try to outperform the market. According to Ghilarducci, analysts get hot sometimes and manage to outperform for a season, but "the statistics show that such hot streaks always end."[8] Also, indexed funds pay less commission to salespeople, and are, thus, cheaper to buy.

Steve added that diversity involves more than the number of stocks or bonds one owns. If I owned stock in 50 companies, but 90% of the value resided in only 4 companies, I would not be adequately diversified. Also, Steve has used active traders from time to time. He said they have more flexibility to help over a short term when market conditions are fluctuating. Again, a professional adviser can evaluate the timing.

Of course, I could put my assets in cash. When my mother-in-law became disabled, the family kept her money in CDs (certificates of deposit) and money market accounts. The problem with each of these is they pay a lower interest (1.5% at the time of this writing) and cannot be accessed early without a substantial penalty. However, they are relatively safe. If bought at a FDIC bank, CDs are insured up to $300,000. The same can't be said for stocks or bonds.

The experts also mentioned annuities, which are popular products for retirees who do not have a pension. With an annuity, you pay the insurance company (that's who sells them) a set amount, say $200,000, and the company writes you an agreed upon monthly check for life. People who are afraid they will outlive their money, and who are afraid they might dip too often into their 401K, like annuities.

Ghilarducci, Solin and Jason recommended immediate, fixed annuities. They are fixed because they pay the same amount each month, and they are immediate because they start paying shortly after the contract is signed. While these plans have differences, they are fairly straightforward and easy to understand. One can choose a joint-annuity which pays until both spouses are deceased, and there is an annuity that guarantees returns for beneficiaries even if the policy owner dies—a ten years certain option. Theoretically, without a stipulation like this, one could die a few months after buying the annuity and heirs would not get anything. That is the downside to annuities. They are not inheritable, and they cannot be accessed in an emergency.

On the other hand, all my authors said not to buy deferred variable or equity-indexed annuities. The reasons were complex. According to Solin and Jason, these plans generate fat commissions for the salesperson but fail to deliver on their promises. Suffice it to say that chapter 18 of Solin's book and chapter 10 of Jason's kept me from considering these types of annuities. Steve concurred. "They are too expensive, and you can do better," he said. Besides, I had my teacher retirement to provide fixed monthly income so an annuity was not something I needed.

The authors warned against other unwise investments. Most did not like reverse mortgages—a plan where you give ownership of your house to a company who in return writes you a monthly check for life. Ghilarducci said these plans tend to have high, up-front fees and interest rates.[9] She pointed out that AARP and consumer protection agencies also do not back the concept. At the least, said Ghilarducci, talk with a financial adviser before purchasing a reverse mortgage.

Which brings up a whole other discussion. It seems that elder fraud is a popular cottage industry in America. According to Jason, AARP has an entire section on their website listing resources to educate consumers on the subject.[10] And meeting with a financial advisor is no guarantee against getting swindled because a portion of them (some with phony credentials) are themselves swindlers.

So most of the experts had a list of questions I could ask potential advisors. Kinder wanted me to know if the person was local, certified as a CFP or RLP, operated by fee only (as opposed to commissions) and whether he or she had a fiduciary relationship with clients[11] (a legal term that requires the advisor to operate in the best interest of the client). Solin wanted me to make sure funds were held at an independent, well-known custodian like Charles Schwab or Fidelity Investments. If I invested on my own, he wanted me to use well-known fund families, such as Vanguard or T Rowe Price.[12] Julie Jason's list was long and included things like providing disclosure statements, knowing how the advisor was paid and whether he or she provided a referral fee to anyone who sent me their way.[13]

Finally, Steve said I should ask around (friends and

family) and read the reviews (evidently, Google would help). Steve's eyes lit up when he talked of investing. It made me realize that for some, investing could be like starting a business is to me—not just a path to their dream but part of it.

As I concluded the financial part of my research, I was struck with the irony of it. When money was first in my thinking, I was unable and, perhaps, unwilling to tackle the hard issues. But when I put the dream first and saw money as a tool, it all fell into place. Interestingly, I even enjoyed working with budgets and such. But my research wasn't over. I was about to discover other powerful tools for helping one's retirement dreams come true.

SO MANY FRIENDS, SO LITTLE TIME

FEBRUARY 10, 2017

I'M NOT AN RVER, but for those of you who are, I think I get it.

It's not only the wanderlust or the nice rigs (nicer than the hotels I visit). I'm betting the greatest appeal is the camaraderie. When I happen on a group of you at a campsite, I hear the same story. You've been doing this—with the same people—for years.

Makes sense to me. The pleasure of visiting places increases exponentially with the number of good friends who join you. Which brings me to maybe my biggest group of friends.

Trip friends.

Charlotte and I have Santa Fe, New Mexico friends and Ouray, Colorado friends and simply road-trip friends (where the destination doesn't really matter).

For 20 years or so, I've had cycling buddies; mostly we've ridden mountain bikes along the Caprock Canyon Trail outside of Quitaque, Texas, but I've also done some road-bike trips—the longest from El Paso to Canyon (was fun—once).

For the last 10 years, I've done more peak climbing with friends. Real peak climbers call what we do "walk-ups." They're right of course, but walking at 13,000 feet doesn't feel like walking.

And we end up with good stories, which is part of the fun —sharing the adventure, sometimes years later, around food and drink where tales grow bigger with each retelling.

In a perfect world, I'd have a couple of road trips with friends each month—with several week-long adventures over the summer.

So many friends. So little time.

13

THEY'RE HELPING MY DREAMS COME TRUE

"I am not aware of any other factor in medicine that has a greater impact on our survival than the healing power of love and intimacy."

— DEAN ORNISH, M.D.

THE RETIREMENT EXPERTS argued about which investments were best; however, they didn't disagree about something else, something they said every retiree needs as much as money. Apparently, we need friends, and the more the better.

"If you are lucky enough to have good friends, embrace them," wrote Miriam Goodman. "They are literally keeping you alive."[1] Goodman's words were backed by solid research. In *Successful Aging*, Drs. Rowe and Kahn were blunt:

Loneliness breeds both illness and early death... People whose connections with others are relatively strong...live longer. And for people whose relationships to others are fewer and weaker, the risk of death is two to four times as great, irrespective of age.[2]

In 1998, Dr. Dean Ornish wrote *Love & Survival: 8 Pathways to Intimacy and Health.*[3] At the time, he was Clinical Professor of Medicine at the School of Medicine at the University of California. He also held the Bucksbaum Chair in Preventive Medicine at the nonprofit Preventive Medicine Research Institute in Sausalito, California, which he had founded in 1984. Dr. Ornish's research focused on how lifestyle changes could reverse even severe coronary heart disease, without drugs or surgery. And one of these changes had to do with solid friendships. Ornish wrote, "I am not aware of any other factor in medicine that has a greater impact on our survival than the healing power of love and intimacy. Not diet, not smoking, not exercise, not stress, not genetics, not drugs, not surgery."[4]

In addition, writers like Dr. Laura Carstensen pointed out the existential value of friends. They are "what makes life worth living," and people who have them "live more pleasant lives and enjoy better mental health than those [who do not]."[5] Yet, as Leider and Webber explained, we tend to lose friends over time. The ones we made when our children were growing up, the ones we lost through the years because of physical moves (theirs or ours) and now the work friends whom we don't see regularly because of retirement are unavailable to us. "The reality in this new phase of life is that it's all too easy to end up with a wealth of casual acquaintances and a poverty of real friends."[6]

Thus, Leider and Webber recommended forming new kinds of communities of "good friends who genuinely get you and offer you deep friendships."[7] This is what George and Mabel Mead did at Sun City, what Marika and Howard Stone did through their advocacy groups and what I saw my parents do in their 80s when they volunteered to be program leaders in a retirement community. Yet, some of us (maybe most of us) will not have to find new ones. Charlotte and I took mental inventory and found an abundance of old friends with whom we wanted to renew or deepen connections.

In 2013, country music legends Kenny Rogers and Dolly Parton released what, in their minds, would be the last of their many hit duets. It was named, appropriately, "You Can't Make Old Friends."[8] Written by Ryan Hanna King, Caitlyn Smith and Don Schlitz (the latter wrote "The Gambler"), the piece spoke movingly of the kind of relationships unique to old friends (for instance, they can finish each other's stories). I first heard the song a year into retirement, and it struck a nerve. So I forced many of my old friends to listen, too. It's the best way I could find to tell them what they meant to me, and what I hoped to both give to and receive from them in the future.

Actually, it was part of my dream. Whatever I would create or build in life, whatever adventures I would take, whatever pieces I would write or classes I would teach, and whatever things I would provide others—would be done for and with good friends, both new and old.

Still, there was one more discovery on the subject. Leider and Webber recommended creating a "Sounding Board:" five or so friendly, diverse, encouraging (no naysayers allowed) people who would help us plan the retirement transition.[9] Actually, Charlotte and I started the process informally before I read Leider and Webber. Hands down, it's been the best perk of retirement—the times we are spending with good friends. We had some over last night. Three couples, we ate at a favorite TexMex spot, then came to our place for some porchin' (what we call what we do on the front porch).

What did we talk about? Well, adult children and grandchildren—there's always one or two in crisis. No one offers much advice. By this time in life, we know better. Mostly, we listen, and sympathize, and empathize (we've been there, too). And we talk about parents, those still alive and those who are gone (each presents its own happiness and pain). But if you had sat at the bottom of the hill which we overlook, you would not judge this a somber group. The laughter is deep and long—mostly from retelling old stories.

And we talk of dreams—of things we want to do, of places we want to go—sometimes with each other. I haven't brought it up yet, but I will ask them to be my Sounding Board—about my retirement dreams and plans, about writing this book. They'll be honest and supportive, and if you're reading this and receiving the encouragement I hoped for, you'll have my friends to thank.

RETIRED HUSBAND SYNDROME

JULY 23, 2016

RETIRED HUSBAND SYNDROME—THE term was coined in 1984 by Dr. Charles Clifford, who, writing in the *Western Journal of Medicine*, described wives of the newly retired who said things like "I'm going nuts" and "he's under my feet all the time."

Clifford said these women reported "headaches, depression, agitation, palpitations and lack of sleep."

Evidently, the condition is prevalent in Japan, too, where they have their own name for it (*Shujin Zaitaku Sutoresu Shoukougu*), which loosely translates "One's Husband Being at Home Stress Syndrome."

There's even a book about it. Miriam Goodman wrote *Too Much Togetherness* in 2011.

So I decided to address the topic head-on.

"Honey," I asked her. "Do you have retired husband syndrome?"

"What?"

"Am I under your feet all the time?"

"Of course not. — Now run along and make sure you get everything on that list. Don't forget the mail. I'll be at my sister's."

lotte's newly minted rules for fighting (i.e. conflict resolution):

Mike's list:

Each person gets a few minutes to explain his or her point of view without interruption.
Ask questions to clarify the above.
Avoid "you" statements (like "you criticize me too much" or "you blame me for ____." Instead use "I feel" statements (like "I feel like I'm being criticized").
Find shared views, common ground which can be the basis for compromise.
When the issue seems irresolvable, agree to disagree (borrowed this one from Taylor and Mintzer).

Charlotte's list (more practical and relational than mine):

Stop and don't talk. Be silent for a few minutes.
Remember, the person you are talking to is your best friend.
Laugh (don't take yourself too seriously).
When deciding whether to bring up a disagreement, ask, "is this really worth it?"

I don't know if we've used our lists much, but just making them has made us better at "getting to yes together." Finally, I need to say something about the separate space and time issue. What do the experts say about mitigating "too much of him"?

Goodman said we men need to develop more friendships

with other men (to replace those we may have lost leaving the workforce).[9] Where will we find them? C. S. Lewis said that friends, unlike lovers, don't stand face to face but side by side. They're not looking at each other but at a common interest (think of hunting buddies or golf buddies).[10] So it follows if we chase our interests, we'll discover a friend pool. Then, we'll just need to be brave enough to have coffee with someone or share a round of golf.

Goodman went on to advocate a strong connection to the outside world.[11] Preretirement work used to provide this; now, we need something else. Picking up a new gig or two would work, with the added advantage of more money for those dreams. And, if we don't need the bread, there are plenty of volunteer activities for retirees. Be creative. I've asked the summer camp I worked at 40 years ago if they might need a hiking leader some time.

Also, Goodman said men need to practice some alone time, which psychologists and religious leaders say we need anyway. If you've never done this, there are books, even retreats on the subject. In short, Goodman said we must "maintain separate lives,"[12] which I took as regular places to go and things to do individually, not as a couple. This wasn't a hard one for Charlotte and me since we have done so for most of our married life. The only discussion will revolve around schedule—how can my schedule fit with yours? Sounds like an opportunity to practice our fighting rules.

Finally, Sterk said we "should support our partner's dream,"[13] an admonition that seems especially relevant in light of my thesis in this book. I'll be honest. I was halfway through the research (well over a year of reading) before I thought to ask Charlotte what her dreams were. If you think I should be blushing from shame, I am.

THE NEUTRAL ZONE

JANUARY 14, 2017

THE "NEUTRAL ZONE," according to transition expert William Bridges, is where I've been living for the last 229 days.

It's the period between an ending (my days at AC) and a beginning (the new dream, as yet not clearly defined).

Bridges says the neutral zone is the "most tortured" and "treacherous" part of retirement. He calls it "a time of lostness and emptiness before life resumes an intelligible pattern and direction."

And Bridges says the inner transformation that needs to take place during this time can't be rushed. One can't hit the fast-forward button.

Hard stuff for an impatient planner like me. But there is a silver lining. "Take time to get away," writes Bridges.

Hmm. I think I hear Santa Fe calling.

15

ARCTIC TUNDRA, SPANISH SKIRTS AND BUFFALO GRASS

"Fitness cuts your risk of dying; it doesn't get much more 'bottom line' than that."

— Drs. John Rowe and Robert Kahn

Most of the authors I was reading wrote about keeping our bodies healthy as we grow older, and many of them referenced the MacArthur Foundation Study led by Drs. John Rowe and Robert Kahn. And well they should have. Rowe and Kahn changed the way we view aging: "MacArthur research shows us again and again that we need not hope for just added years—we can, and should strive for longer, healthier, more productive lives."[1]

The doctors went on to say that preventive medical studies used to exclude the elderly. Physicians assumed there was no going back. "The horse is out of the barn...it's impossible to change habits that have been ingrained over decades." And even if one could alter his or her lifestyle, "it is unlikely your aged body would respond to improve function and reduce risk."[2] Rightly, Rowe and Kahn identified such thinking as both ageism and a myth.

"Nature is remarkably forgiving," wrote the doctors. "Research shows that it is almost never too late to begin healthy habits such as smoking cessation, sensible diet, exercise, and the like."[3]

And it wasn't too late to benefit from those changes either. For instance, the risk of heart disease "begins to fall almost as soon as you quit smoking—no matter how long you've smoked."[4] "In five years, an ex-smoker is not much more likely to have heart disease than a person who has never smoked."[5] Also, according to the MacArthur study, the same went for other unhealthy practices. "When obese folks lose 10 percent of their body weight, they lower their risk of heart disease, no matter how old they are."[6]

So *stopping* unhealthy practices (smoking or eating too many sweets) could improve one's longevity, yet the finding that caught my eye was that *starting* a new practice, namely regular exercise, could lead to even bigger improvement. "Fitness cuts your risk of dying," wrote the doctors. "It doesn't get much more 'bottom line' than that."[7]

Even more striking, the study found that frequent, moderate exercise could negate other risk factors. "The most fit people, even if they smoke or have high blood pressure, are still at lower risk of death than nonsmokers with normal blood pressures who are couch potatoes."[8] Also, the doctors wrote of exercise's ability to improve mood. I was pretty sure my daily bicycle rides had kept me from a stress-induced disease during our building project. But, according to the study, aerobic exercise was not enough by itself.

Many of us baby boomers remember John F. Kennedy's assassination in Dallas on November 22, 1963. And we remember the assassination attempt on our 40th president, when on March 30, 1981, while leaving the Washington Hilton Hotel, President Ronald Reagan was shot in the chest by John Hinckley Jr. Quick medical attention saved Reagan's life. About eight months later, I watched on TV as he talked to reporters about his rehab. Reagan was showing off his biceps, which, due to prescribed resistance training (pumping iron), had grown dramatically. He was nearing his 71st birthday.

According to Rowe and Kahn, besides increasing muscle size and strength, resistance exercises "also enhance bone strength, limiting the risk of osteoporosis and fractures of the hip, spine and wrist." And, once more, it's never too late to start. "Even the oldest-old respond well to resistance training. Their muscles grow in size and strength much as younger people's do." The doctors referenced a man named Irving who had begun weight training at 87. At 89, he was more active than he had been in years. " Irving uses all five weight machines in the gym—leg presses, leg extensions, leg curls, chest presses, and the triceps machine. He trains three times a week, and does three sets of eight repetitions on each machine."[9]

The authors of *Younger Next Year*, Chris Crowley and Dr. Henry Lodge, would say that Irving was "functionally younger" than his biological age. His exercise routine was more indicative of someone in his 60s. Lodge, a 46-year-old board-certified internist, and Crowley, his 70-year-old patient, wrote their 2004 book to show how retirees like Crowley could put more quality into the quantity of years left them. Dr. Lodge was frustrated because his older patients "had had good medical care but not...great health care." Their illnesses resulted from "30-year problems of lifestyle, not disease."[10]

So, borrowing from the findings of the MacArthur Study, Crowley and Lodge laid out a rigorous plan: exercise six days of every week for the rest of your life and include at least four days of aerobics. They recommended outside activities like biking and swimming and inside things like stationary bikes, treadmills, elliptical machines and stair climbers. An encouraging part of their plan was the value of light aerobic exercise: distance, not speed. "You become more fit with harder exercise, but you gain more endurance and general healthiness with prolonged light exercise" (defined as walking at an easier pace).[11] Do this, said Crowley and Lodge, and "most of us can be functionally younger every year for the next five or even ten years."[12]

Although I had been exercising regularly for some time (mostly bicycling and hiking), I took it up a notch after reading *Younger Next Year*. I turned in my stationary machine for a spinner bike, and I found more resistance training I could do apart from the free weights and machines in a gym —one can do dips on a pair of bar stools, pull-ups on a mounted bar, and push-ups on, well, any hard surface. The point is I had such dreams, and it would be sad to see them ruined by something I could change. As Dr. Lodge pointed out, none of us can avoid one day succumbing to disease or accident, but we can contribute to the quality of the life we will experience before then.

By the way, I was researching for me, but I knew one day I would want to share this with others, and I wondered if exercise works for all retirees. What about those with serious medical conditions? So I googled it, and the experts were adamant. According to a professor at the University of Washington Medical School in Seattle, for those with significant heart disease, "physical activity can strengthen your heart muscle and help you manage blood pressure and cholesterol levels."[13] Similarly, Mayo Clinic staff wrote that exercise is "a drug-free approach to lowering high blood pressure."[14] And the American Cancer Society listed ways regular exercise can help *"during* cancer treatment" (italics are mine).[15]

Finally, in order to be successful, Crowley said I had to join a gym. He had several reasons, things like the camaraderie and energy of a group and the advice of strength training experts, but I wasn't buying it—not for me, anyway. I agreed with the place part—a regular place probably helps regular exercise. But my place wasn't indoors (not always). When I think of fitness, I visualize the valleys of arctic tundra surrounding the mountain peaks in New Mexico and Colorado (this thick mat of grass and wildflower grows only inside the arctic circle and above tree line in the rest of the world), or I imagine the Spanish skirts of the Palo Duro (multicolored, striated rocks on the steep ridges above the canyon's many gorges), or I see buffalo grass (endless waves of it alongside the long, flat stretches of West Texas highways).

Whether I am on foot or on my mountain bike, this is where I like to exercise. And it's why I exercise. It is part of the dream—not just so I can stay in shape to do the good stuff, but because it is the good stuff, a principle that applies to another healthy activity—lifelong learning.

THE DUMAFLACHE IN THE DRAWER

AUGUST 5, 2016

WHILE IT IS true that young people have sharper vision, better hearing, quicker reaction times and better short-term memory than seniors, Dr. Rowe says we can compensate for all of these.

The lead doctor in the MacArthur Foundation study on aging goes on to say we can do things to promote strong mental function. Things like regular physical activity, a strong social support system and belief in "one's ability to handle what life has to offer" (Rowe calls this "self-efficacy") help seniors maintain "sharp mental ability."

That's encouraging because I get the short-term memory thing. Why is it I can remember the phone numbers of childhood friends from the 50s (Swatzell is 3075, Scott is 3010 and Susan is 4444) but not the name of the dumaflache I want Charlotte to bring me?

Me: "You know, the dumaflache. It's in the drawer next to the hammer."

Her: "You want what?"

Me: "The dumaflache. You know, it tightens things."

Her: "Do you mean the pliers?"

Me: "Yeah, that's it. Bring me the dumaflache."

Maybe I need to work on self-efficacy.

_____

16

WE JUST KNOW STUFF

"The brain is like a muscle and can be pumped at any age."

— Barbara Strauch

According to the MacArthur study, older people worry excessively about losing mental abilities. Specifically, they are afraid of being placed in a nursing home. But, said Drs. Rowe and Kahn, "only 5 percent of people over the age of 65 live in nursing homes, and that percentage has been falling for at least 10 years."[1] I, too, worried about mental agility. Like most of my 60-something friends, my memory isn't what it used to be—at least short-term memory. Ask me trivia from the 60s (who played Jed Clampett in the Beverly Hillbillies?), and I'm all over it (Buddy Epsen, of course); however, if you ask me the name of the new couple coming to church (who have introduced themselves more than once), good luck.

The MacArthur study did find that older people score lower on memory tests than younger folks, and it's the short-term stuff where it shows up. Rowe and Kahn called it a failure of "explicit memory"—like the inability to recall a specific name on demand—that's it, Jerry and Kay, the new folks sitting across from me in Sunday school. The good news is that "working memory"—the "learned routines on which all of us rely in our daily lives—show little decline with age."[2] So I might forget the name of the implement, but I still know how to use pliers to tighten a loose nut.

Deborah Burke, a neuroscientist at Pomona College in California, called these types of memory loss (forgetting a name we should know) "Tots" or "tip-of-the-tongue" incidents.[3] It's right there; you just can't say it. Burke said Tots begin to creep into our lives as early as the mid-30s. Barbara Strauch, an award winning journalist and author of *The Secret Life of the Grown-up Brain*, said we also have trouble with "episodic memory"—recent events like a meal eaten or a book read yesterday. Burke explained that our problem is not storage but retrieval: "It's like trying to find the right book in a well-stocked library."[4]

And there's another issue. We have a distraction problem, which explains why, when building our house, I kept turning my pickup truck at wrong streets—I was sure it was early Alzheimer's. But Strauch said it's because "our front lobes don't block out irrelevant details," creating what she called an "inhibitory deficit." Older brains, she said, "let distracting and irrelevant scene information sneak in."[5] It's probably the reason this book has been more difficult than a longer Ph.D. dissertation completed in my 40s. Such projects require sifting through a lot of irrelevant information.

Strauch wrote that memory and cognitive functions in general slow down a bit as we age. However, it's not as bad as once thought. "For years people in aging science studied only those in nursing homes, hardly the center of high powered inductive reasoning."[6] Even doctors once thought that dementia was inevitable. Yet while its risk certainly increases with age, dementia is not normal aging. It is a specific disease. "If we maintain a normal path of aging without major illnesses," wrote Strauch, "our brains can stay in relatively good shape."[7]

And now that studies are dealing with better samples, researchers have found that not only are declines overstated; gains have been understated. The older brain actually has its advantages. It's better at recognizing patterns and seeing connections; it's better able to "predict and navigate life."[8] Besides, as one scientist told Strauch, "we just know stuff."[9]

I knew my dreams would depend on a healthy mind as well as body so I wondered if I could do something to keep it sharp. Yes, said Drs. Rowe and Kahn. Strenuous physical activity helps maintain high cognitive function.[10] In addition, training and practice (mostly associating strategies), social support (good friends) and something they called "self-efficacy" helps. The doctors defined the latter as "a person's belief in his or her own ability to handle various situations."[11] So a can-do spirit is good for the brain.

Strauch agreed. "The brain is like a muscle and can be pumped at any age,"[12] she wrote. It's called "neuroplasticity"—the brain can and does change. The myelin (white tissue that carries messages) can build and reroute (as when someone has a stroke or brain injury).[13] What will do that? Strauch mentioned physical exercise, leisure activities, cognitive stimulation and education. Studies have shown that learning a new language, learning to play a new instrument and even certain video games are helpful.[14] I finally had it: permission to dust off my Marine Band harmonica.

Strauch pointed out that one of the best things we have going for us is something that seems to happen naturally. It's called bilateralization.[15] Research has shown that older people use both the right and left hemisphere of their brains —at the same time. It's like lifting a chair with two hands rather than one (the idea is that the young use only one hemisphere at a time—because they can). So "while younger people may have a processing speed advantage, older people are better at solving multi-faceted complex tasks, such as making financial decisions."[16]

Finally, according to the MacArthur study, "Education was the strongest predictor of sustained mental function. People with more years of schooling are more likely to maintain high cognitive function."[17] The observation led researchers to two conclusions. One, early education contributed to good "brain circuitry," which was still in place 50 or more years later. And, two, early education set "a pattern of intellectual activities," which was continuing into retirement years and still maintaining—maybe even creating —good mental health, which made me think of another trend among modern retirees.

"There is a burgeoning movement that *Newsweek* has called the 'golden age on campus,' where hundreds of thousands of people in their Third Chapters are moving to communities in order to be in close proximity to institutions of higher education," wrote Sara Lightfoot.[18] Thankfully, it seems these retirees will find a hearty welcome from academia. In a November, 2016 article, thepennyhoarder.com claimed all 50 states in the U.S. offer free or reduced tuition.[19] Following are some of the listings (all are direct quotes from the website):

Alabama seniors can attend any two-year institution within the state completely free.

California State University waives all tuition and dramatically reduces campus fees for residents age 60 or older.

The Florida college system waives application, tuition and student fees for those age 60 and above, but colleges will award no credit and will grant admission on a space-available basis.

Tuition is waived for senior citizens attending North Carolina community colleges.

My state was not quite as generous: Texas law allows students 65 and up the opportunity to take six credit hours of undergraduate or graduate courses for free at public universities.

And so it went. All 50 states gave some kind of financial break to people like me. And, by the way, I was interested. A Ph.D. (my degree) gives one a lot of information in a very small area, but there is so much more I want to know. Surely, I thought, some university has an online class on Texas trail drives.

There was more. If you like to combine education and travel (and who wouldn't?), there's the Road Scholar program. Begun in 1975 as Elderhostel, today, Road Scholar offers 5,500 learning adventures and serves more than 100,000 participants annually. According to their website, their programs combine travel and education on a range of topics in every state in the U.S., in 150 countries and onboard ships on rivers and oceans worldwide.[20] The 14-day hiking tour in the Swiss Alps got my attention.

Colleges and universities call it lifelong learning, and it's the fastest growing movement on campuses around the U.S. Lifelong learning classes are more for personal enrichment. There are no tests, no homework and the fees are low.

At the University of North Carolina, Asheville, participants 50 and over pay $75 for an annual membership, then about $70 each semester for as many classes as they can cram into their schedules. And these aren't what I thought of as typical "senior college" courses (you know, things like how to use a computer or navigate Social Security). When Charlotte and I visited during the Spring of 2017, offerings included "How to Think like a Philosopher," "Bob Dylan and the Boomers," "William Faulkner's *The Sound and the Fury*" and "Spring Wildflower Hikes in the Blue Ridge." We sat in on a course taught by a retired English professor called "Folk Music Revival in America." The two-hour class included YouTube videos of groups like The Kingston Trio. There was lively group discussion, and our teacher even got out his banjo.

In 2018, there were 100s (perhaps over 1000) of these life-long learning experiences across the U.S. UNC Asheville's program is associated with the Osher Institute for Lifelong Learning (OLLI), a consortium of over 120 colleges and universities, and widely considered standard bearers in the field. Begun in 2001 by the Bernard Osher Foundation (and funded by the wealthy San Francisco businessman), OLLIs operate in all 50 states and the District of Columbia.[21]

So I would have plenty of opportunity to keep learning, an activity the experts said would keep my mind healthy, but the corollary was even better. What we learn can be its own reward. Researching this book had taught me how to identify my dreams, how to deal with past traumas that threaten those dreams, how to finance the dreams—I could go on. Older minds engaged in lifelong learning have acquired what the Bible calls wisdom. We're better equipped to navigate life (and to help others do the same). In short, we just know stuff.

ON GRATEFULNESS

JULY 8, 2016

INSTALLED COUNTERTOPS YESTERDAY, and the bricklayers finished an inside fireplace—both beautiful work. I'm thankful for skilled craftsmen. Am watching one of our famous West Texas sunrises as I write these words, and I'm thankful for it, too.

At a friend's suggestion, last spring I started every prayer with 10 things for which I was thankful.

Don't do it with every prayer now, nor every day, but when I do, I'm finding that gratefulness is powerful stuff.

Don't know if it makes my prayers more effective, but it certainly helps me.

Makes me more positive, less critical; more confident, less fearful; more relaxed, less uptight. I smile more when I'm grateful.

And, interestingly enough, I find more things to put in this blog.

17

HOPE WORKS

"Hope is not just a feel-good emotion. Research shows it connected to success in things ranging from academic achievement to sports to science to business."

— DR. SCOTT BARRY KAUFMAN

I GUESS I knew from the beginning that one needed more than a healthy body and mental acuity to navigate retirement. One can be smart and fit and still struggle with inferiority, or guilt, or fear, or helplessness, or worry, or fear, or depression (the list is long). Similarly, a dream by itself will not motivate. One, also, must believe that he or she has a reasonable expectation of achieving that dream. My research had led me to hope.

Confidence

In the last chapter, I learned that a can-do spirit is good for the grown-up brain. Rowe and Kahn called it "self-efficacy."

It's the idea that yes, you can teach an old dog new tricks, and this mutt is ready to give it a try. Rowe and Kahn's research demonstrated the reality: Older minds can "absorb new data" and "acquire new skills." And the gains are "significant" and "permanent."[1]

A self-efficacious retiree believes this and will not give up because of a false sense of inadequacy. "Many studies have shown that this form of self-esteem leads to improved performance of many kinds, including persistence in solving cognitive problems, success in mathematical performance, and mastery of computer procedures."[2] Translation: just because fulfilling some of my retirement dreams (i.e. writing this book) seem harder than anything I've done before, doesn't mean they can't happen. And believing that is itself half the battle won.

Optimism

Optimism is another corollary to hope. In this case, it seems that possessing this trait is made easier by age. "Scientists are finding that, around middle age, we begin to adopt a rosier worldview," wrote Barbara Strauch in *The Secret Life of the Grown-up Brain*. Strauch went on to say that, contrary to popular stereotypes of grumpy older people, "our brains may be set up to make us more optimistic as we age."[3]

Strauch referenced John Gabrieli, a neuroscientist and head of a brain imaging lab at MIT, who said our amygdalae (he called it the Homeland Security Department of the brain) reacts less to negative things as we age. "Our brains, in some automatic, preconscious way, begin to, as they say, accentuate the positive and eliminate the negative."[4]

Gabrieli said the condition might have been caused by normal evolution, a phenomenon called the "Grandmother

Hypothesis." "Humans and primates that had helpful, living grandmothers in their group lived longer."[5] I thought of my own Granna who was the first to compliment the stories of "Jim and Clem," my eight-year-old attempt at writing. I also thought of a newspaper column I had written in the '90s. Referencing a 1964-1965 study by Harvard's Robert Rosenthal, I had written that elementary teachers who were told their students were gifted and talented found they were just that. After teaching these "special" children for a semester (who in reality were chosen randomly and no more special than their peers), scores on standardized IQ tests were higher than the control group. Thus, Rosenthal's work showed the results were caused by more than seeing what one wants to see (the so-called "halo effect").[6] Indeed, people do tend to live up or down to our expectations of them. Strauch's research made me think that, perhaps, the same works for self-expectations. Maybe, as retirees, we first *see* the positives in us; then, somehow, we help make them happen.

Gratefulness

Another attitude that research showed correlated with optimism was gratitude. So said Robert Emmons, a professor of psychology at the University of California, Davis and author of *Thanks!: How the New Science of Gratitude Can Make You Happier*. In a 2010 article, Dr. Emmons listed a host of benefits that follow those who practice gratitude. Among them are a stronger immune system, lower blood pressure, better sleep (Emmons said "don't count sheep; count blessings"), more joy and pleasure, and more happiness and optimism.[7]

He had me at sleep. Emmons said that in order for me to experience gratitude, I had to one, acknowledge the presence of goodness in my life; two, recognize that the source of this goodness lay, at least partially, outside myself ("one can be grateful to other people, to God, to animals, but never to oneself"),[8] and, three, I needed to realize that the gift(s) I received was/were (at least to a degree) undeserved ("gratitude implies humility").

Emmons recommended keeping a gratitude journal, which, he said, could mean listing "just five things for which you're grateful every week."[9] I liked the idea of a short list; it passed the self-efficacy test. I thought it something I actually could do. I practiced this regularly in my "neutral zone" days, when anxiety was at a climax, and was surprised how it made me not only calmer (the sleep part) but more hopeful. Only now, two years later, am I realizing why. Gratitude is hope looking backward. The things for which one is grateful now are things for which one was once hopeful, and the "coincidence" does not go unnoticed. We get it. Hope works.

Hope Itself

"Cutting edge science shows that hope, at least as defined by psychologists, matters a lot," wrote Scott Barry Kaufman, a professor at Columbia. Dr. Kaufman said it isn't good enough to have goals (read "dreams"); one has to get closer to those goals—and as a result, more hopeful. "Hope is not just a feel-good emotion," he wrote; "research shows it connected to success in things ranging from academic achievement to sports to science to business."[10]

Dr. Kaufman cited the groundbreaking work of positive psychologist Charles Snyder, who, in 1991, came up with a thing called "Hope Theory." According to Snyder, hope consists of "agency and pathways." Kaufman put it like this: "hope involves the will to get there, and different ways to get there." Snyder developed a hope scale (a test) that would measure how hopeful respondents were both in "agency" and "pathways." I completed the test (it's short, and you can take it online). My take on it is that "agency" has to do with a positive (hopeful) view of one's life. To determine my agency trait, I responded to statements like "I energetically pursue my goals," and "I meet the goals that I set for myself." The agency trait seems to be created by one's past, good parenting styles, for instance. However, pathways seem more existential, something we can work on now.[11]

The "pathways" statements in Snyder's test were more about strategies one uses when in a tough spot—"I can think of many ways to get out of a jam," and "there are lots of ways around any problem." The pathways trait seemed to relate to two other hope corollaries which researchers had suggested: creativity (Cameron) and resiliency (Schlossberg). The first we need to explore all the possibilities for getting to our dreams, and the second, to keep trying when the first, or third, or fifth way doesn't pan out.

Of course, hope is not a modern concept. The Bible mentions it frequently. In his *Expository Dictionary of New Testament Words*, scholar W. E. Vine said the primary Greek word for hope (*elpis*) means a "favorable and confident expectation" that has to do with the "unseen and the future."[12] Remember, I told you that the courage I needed to pursue my dream took more than I had to give? Well, here's the explanation. Vine would say I was expecting a favorable intervention from an unseen God (I'm not sure about the "confident" part; I often felt pretty shaky: "Help Thou my unbelief"). But the voicing of such a prayer is a hopeful idea all by itself. Dreams impossible to us are not impossible to the God of hope (see Matthew 19:26 and Romans 15:13).

In turning to biblical hope, I was on familiar ground. My first degree was in theology. I reminded myself that, for me, daily Bible study would be a necessity in retirement. As the Apostle Paul put it: "Faith comes by hearing and hearing by the word of God" (Romans 10:17 – NKJV).

I end this chapter with an observation. Hope always has an object. One has to hope in something (or someone). Thinking about hope had made me think of hope producers. The Bible was one, but there were many more—books, movies, music, art, nature, friends—things that drew attention to the object(s) of my hope and, thus, made hope stronger. I would need to return to these often. (For an example of one of my hope producers, see Appendix B: How C. S. Lewis Made Me Love Heaven.)

MURKY DREAMS

JULY 5, 2016

TRIM CARPENTERS FINISHED YESTERDAY. They worked Saturday and on the 4th.

Suppose it had anything to do with those double-fudge brownies Charlotte baked them?

Amazing what happens toward the end of a building project. Little things (like window sills and baseboards) make all the difference.

Suddenly, the murky dreams of design and long hours of foundation work begin to take shape—it is going to be as beautiful as imagined (maybe better).

For one still in the murky-dream-phase of retirement, this is encouraging stuff.

18

SOMETHING FROM NOTHING

"Creativity, like play, can turn an old person into a young person."

— Dr. George Vaillant

"CREATIVITY," according to Dr. George Vaillant, "is absolutely necessary for someone to be healthy."[1] Vaillant, a practicing psychiatrist and professor at Harvard Medical School, was commenting on findings of the Harvard Study of Adult Development. This landmark project is important because it was the first longevity study on aging. Its subjects were men who were born in the 1920s, graduated from Harvard in the 1940s and were interviewed every seven years thereafter until researchers published the results in 2002.

Unlike other studies, the Harvard project wanted to know what went right, not wrong, in the aging process. And, according to their data, part of what goes right with those who age well is the presence and practice of creativity. "Creativity like play, can turn an old person into a young person," wrote Vaillant.[2]

Historically, it's interesting that Vaillant even associated creativity with retirees. For in the first half of the 20th century, academic opinion had been shaped by Sir William Osler, a renown Canadian physician and one of four founding faculty at Baltimore's Johns Hopkins University. In a 1905 address titled "The Fixed Period," Osler proposed two "fixed ideas" on aging.[3] One dealt with the "comparative uselessness" of men over 40. Osler argued that world history showed most of mankind's great achievements had been accomplished by people under 40.[4] He didn't mention that life expectancy during most of that period was also at or near 40.

Osler's second fixed idea referred to the uselessness of men over 60.[5] The doctor said it would be of "incalculable benefit" to all of us if folks over 60 would just stop working.[6] Osler, 56 at the time, left the U.S. that year to become the Chair of Medicine at Christ Church Oxford, a post he held until his death—at 70.

Later in the century, many would challenge Osler's ideas, including Dean Keith Simonton, a psychologist at the University of California, Davis. Simonton showed that, although there was a gradual decline of creativity after middle age, it was "a mild decline, not a sharp falling off."[7] Simonton also produced an impressive list of authors, composers, even scientists who had produced their greatest works after 60, among them the artist Goethe who put the finishing touches on his *Faust* at age 83, the astronomer Laplace who completed his seminal work *Celestial Mechanics* when he was 79, and the chemist Chevreul who began studying gerontology in his 90s and published his last scientific paper at 102. Wrote Simonton, "People can produce masterpieces up to the day they die."[8]

So what exactly is creativity? Mirriam-Webster was not much help. They say creativity is "the ability to create." Vaillant was better. He said creativity is "putting something into the world that was not there before."[9] Similarly, Julia Cameron (*It's Never Too Late to Begin Again: Discovering Creativity and Meaning at Midlife and Beyond*) wrote, creativity is "making something from nothing."[10] Known for her work with uninspired artists and playwrights—she excels at "unblocking" one's creativity—Cameron believes we are "meant" to be creative. In her view, God, who is creative, instills creativity in all creatures. "When we open ourselves to our creativity, we open ourselves to the creator's creativity within us... Creativity is God's gift to us. Using our creativity is our gift back to God."[11]

So how do we open ourselves to creativity? Cameron has her clients do four things:[12] Morning Pages is what she calls stream-of-consciousness writing (two to three pages, hand-written, not typed), which one is to do every day. Any subject is okay. The point is to write what is on your mind. Two, an Artist Date is something you do weekly. It should be fun and somewhat unusual—not something one does regularly. You must go alone for this activity—indeed, all of her steps are done individually. Three, she wants us to walk daily. The emphasis is on noticing and enjoying nature; it's not a fitness thing. And, four, Cameron's book leads readers through writing a life memoir. She suggests dividing your years by seven and writing weekly thoughts in each section. Her questions for this exercise make excellent writing prompts as she has us notice sounds, smells, specific visuals and attitudes. She also wants us to notice what we love because, she believes, what you love tells you who you are.[13]

As a writer, I had done free-writing and had written a memoir. Also, I've taken regular walks most of my life. I was already aware of how much these activities stimulated creativity. But the Artist Date was a new thing. She wanted it to be fun; however, her examples—visiting bookstores, plant nurseries, pet stores or going to a zoo or aviary—didn't push my button. Then, Cameron called it "assigned play," and I was on board. I spent a good hour writing down things I'd like to do, most of them childhood loves or dreams. The only thing is most (like snow skiing or paddling a canoe) are going to take a little longer than Cameron had in mind.

Still, Cameron's activities are just preparation. They are there to "unblock" our creativity. The creativity it unlocks seems to go best with our post retirement identity and calling. So I'm using creativity to design spaces both inside and out of our house. It's also what leads me to write these chapters you are reading. They are not exactly "something out of nothing." I'm using material from other creative folks. What I'm trying to do (and this is the creative part) is choose relevant parts and arrange them into something that will (pick one) create meaning, inspiration, practical help, and, always, joy—for me and for the reader.

I'll be honest. Too often I get bogged down. When that happens, I feel not only unproductive but lazy and bored. Cameron told me to call it what it is, not laziness but fear. "What we really are is frightened," she wrote. "We are afraid to take a risk, afraid to try something new."[14] But it's not just trying something new I'm afraid of. It's that what I write won't be good, or not good enough. This is where Cameron was once again convicting. It seems I could use a good dose of humility. "Dreams remain dreams and nothing more when we insist on their being fulfilled instantly and perfectly."[15] Bingo. Creativity can create something out of nothing, but only if one is patient enough to suffer through imperfect, flawed starts. I hope you do better with that one than I have.

IN PRAISE OF SPONTANEITY

AUGUST 10, 2016

DID two things yesterday that aren't normal for me.

First, I got up at 7:30 a.m., which is over an hour later than normal—because I've been waking with the sun and this morning was overcast.

And two, last night we went to dinner with friends, then lingered for an hour or two, just visiting. What's unusual about that? It was a Tuesday.

Before retiring, I would have done neither. Waking has not been determined by the sun but an alarm clock. And leisurely nights with friends were possible only on weekends, and, then, only if I was caught up on grading.

I know we need clocks and schedules to get things done, but I wonder what we lose in using them.

Maybe rest—I'm guessing my body is a better judge of how much sleep I need than is my clock.

And maybe spontaneity—It's the difference in smiling for the camera and smiling because you can't help it.

Schedules make sure I do things on time; spontaneity has me do them on purpose.

19

BECOMING DANGEROUS MEN AND WOMEN

"Some work of noble note, may yet be done,
Not unbecoming men that strove with gods."

— ALFRED LORD TENNYSON – "ULYSSES"

IN READY TO PULL THE *Retirement Trigger*, financial planner Mary Sterk wrote, "What legacy, if any, would you like to leave? What is important to you about the impact you leave on this world?"[1] It's Sterk's version of Kinder's vision questions to determine one's dream, and it's a topic on which most retirement books touch. Julia Cameron, sounding much like Kinder, offered five exploratory questions:[2]

"I would like to be remembered as…"
"I wish I could leave…"
"A person whose legacy inspires me is…"
"As a child, I dreamed of…"
"One way I am already leaving a legacy is…"

Just what is legacy? According to Webster, it's "a gift by will, especially of money or other personal property." Meg Newhouse (*Legacies of the Heart: Living a Life that Matters*) has a broader definition. Legacy is "anything, tangible or intangible, of any size...that we intentionally or unintentionally give or leave behind." It is "the imprint of our lives that endures in some form."[3]

I will return to Newhouse. She has insightful things to say about the non-financial things we leave for others, but first, I need to start with the legal aspect of legacy, something which all financial planners, lawyers, priests, pastors and just about every other authority agrees with: you and I need a will. And, yet, according to a 2016 Gallop poll, the majority of adult Americans do not have the legal document (44%, down from 51% in 1990). One would think the numbers get better with age, and they do. Gallop said 68% of those over 65 have wills, but that was down from 78% in 2005.[4] I guess we baby boomers are expecting to take it with us, which would be funny if it weren't so sad.

If you die intestate (without a will), it is indeed sad for your descendants, for as any attorney will tell you, the state in which you live has a will for you if you haven't made one yourself. And it, most likely, is not what you would want. Kate Ashford, writing in *Forbes*, listed several unintended consequences of dying intestate.[5] Pulling from several real-life "horror stories," she showed how the predicament can cause sibling in-fighting, children who get nothing, a life partner without legal standing, life insurance ending up in the wrong hands, heirs unable to locate stuff and unnecessary, exorbitant taxes and legal fees.

Charlotte and I had a will, but it had not been updated in some time. So I read Deborah Layton's *The Everything Wills & Estate Planning Book*, then made appointments with an accountant and lawyer. The process was surprisingly painless and not as expensive as I expected. Maybe the best result was that it led to a time when we could have "the talk" with children about the will and other end-of -life stuff. Interestingly, the kids seemed to appreciate it, too, probably because they had heard first-hand some of the horror stories.

No discussion of legacy is complete without mentioning Erick Erickson, a famous 20th century psychoanalyst known for his study of human life stages. Especially important for my research were his concepts of generativity and "Keeper of the Meaning," the fourth and fifth of his six life "tasks." Generativity is the practice of healthy seniors giving to and guiding the next generations. Erickson said these acts required humility and unselfishness.[6] Commenting on the first of these, George Vaillant wrote, "successful aging requires continuing to learn new things and continuing to take people in." Valliant went on to say that those who could not list things they had learned from their children were not practicing generativity.[7] The thought resonated with this retired professor. A healthy dose of humility is necessary for both teacher and student. Addressing the second issue (unselfishness), Newhouse quoted a Greek proverb: "A society grows great when its elders plant trees under whose shade they shall never sit."[8]

The idea of "Keeper of the Meaning" is that people my age should be "wise judges" who can bring the perspective of history into the present. Vaillant wrote, "only the old can make the past come alive for the next generation."[9] I thought of the summer camp where I worked 50 plus years ago, and I remembered the rich legacy left by its founder. Present day camp counselors know almost nothing about Uncle John, as we called him. And they will be poorer for it unless we tell his story.

But what if the next generation doesn't want to be mentored? What if they don't want to listen to the wisdom of their elders? I think Erickson would point to his two requirements. We must earn a hearing with open minds (humility) and giving hearts (unselfishness). Note to self: Appreciate if you want to be appreciated. Listen if you want to be listened to. Back to Meg Newhouse. An educator, career and life coach, Newhouse specialized in what she called "positive aging."[10] In her book on legacies, the best stuff dealt with non-material and non-financial gifts to one's progeny. On the non-material side, she wrote of things like forgiveness, which she said benefits the forgiver even more than the forgiven. Newhouse brought up Ira Byock, a M.D. specializing in palliative care for those with advanced medical conditions. Dr. Byock said that people at this life stage need to say four things to their closest friends and family (His book is called *The Four Things That Matter Most*). These are "Please forgive me," "I forgive you," "Thank you," and "I love you."[11] It seemed like a good list for all of us, not just those in hospice care. Anyway, I made a mental note to say these more often. It would be a good start to my non-material legacy.

My parents left me some immaterial legacies. From my dad, I received a legacy of generosity. From Mom, one of hope and resilience. After a successful career in real estate, Dad lost everything (including his home) in an Arizona market collapse, but he still retired the next year at age 60. He and Mom moved as planned to their dream spot in New Mexico. Later, because of Mom's health issues, they located closer to family in Texas. Sure, Dad had to work some part-time gigs, but he never complained. In fact, he seemed to enjoy them. And they did all the things they dreamed of doing—traveling, hanging out with family and friends. In short, for 25 years my parents lived a happy, fulfilling retirement.

So, in his later years, Dad had no money with which to be generous, but he was generous with his encouragement and praise, gifts that helped me get through grad school. In her early 60s, Mom developed rheumatoid arthritis, but she refused to let it keep her from productive living. In her later years, she scheduled rides for cancer patients to see their doctors, and, crippled hands notwithstanding, she created hand-made cards for our Christmas and birthdays.

As to non-financial, material gifts, Newhouse had a number of creative ideas for passing our "imprint" on to others, like writing a memoir, or creating a recipe book, or putting together a photo album, things which, it seemed to me, would be useful gifts now as well as after one has passed.

Most importantly, Newhouse linked legacy to life purpose, which she defined as "our reason for being; our calling or vocation that expresses our deepest values, passions, and unique gifts."[12] The words reminded me of Os Guinness and his comment on T. E. Lawrence. It's our calling which causes us to dream with eyes wide open, which, in turn, makes us dangerous men and dangerous women. Why should young adults be the only ones who optimistically and boldly attempt to change the world or at least their own worlds?

The question made me think of the 17-year-old me who passionately held such thoughts, as well as the 70-year-old who still does (as, I'm guessing, you do, too). Whether interacting with grandchildren or starting a new gig, or traveling to a new place, or doing something to improve life for society as a whole, I want to be dangerous. I want these days to matter.

The attitude is captured by Alfred Lord Tennyson in his

poem "Ulysses."[13] You remember Ulysses (his Greek name was Odysseus) as the hero of Homer's epic poem, *The Odyssey*. Ulysses was the Arnold Schwarzenegger of ancient Greek fiction, a powerful and successful warrior, admired by men and loved by women. Writing in 1833, Tennyson had readers imagine a retired Ulysses. He no longer does what made him famous (his battles and geographic adventures), but rules his island kingdom of Ithaca by enacting "Unequal laws to a savage race, / That hoard, and sleep, and feed, and know not me." Ulysses feels unappreciated and useless, like a discarded sword: "How dull it is to pause, to make an end, / To rust unburnish'd, not to shine in use!"

But Ulysses has a plan. He will leave his son Telemachus to govern the island while he takes one last grand adventure with his former comrades in arms. Like him, these men are well past their prime, but Ulysses reminds them they still can do something special, worthy of the men they once were:

> *Old age hath yet his honour and his toil;*
> *Death closes all: but something ere the end,*
> *Some work of noble note, may yet be done,*
> *Not unbecoming men that strove with gods.*

So Ulysses urges his friends to make one more sailing voyage, to "seek a newer world." Sure, he says, we may sail beyond the sunset and drop off of a flat earth ("the gulfs will wash us down"), but we still have it in us to be dangerous men. His conclusion is an inspiration to all who feel the same.

The best is yet to be

Tho' much is taken, much abides; and tho'
We are not now that strength which in old days
Moved earth and heaven, that which we are, we are;
One equal temper of heroic hearts,
Made weak by time and fate, but strong in will
To strive, to seek, to find, and not to yield.

WIDE OPEN SPACES

AUGUST 17, 2016

HIKED in the Palo Duro again today. It's one of my retirement perks—to experience regularly pleasures once available only sporadically.

Anyway, looking northeast where Highway 207 crosses the canyon at its widest, I was reminded how much I love wide open spaces (no, this blog is not about the Dixie Chicks).

Not sure why. Maybe it's inherited from frontier ancestors who saw in them wide possibilities, wide opportunities, maybe a wideness to hope itself.

I hope they do that for me.

And, whether in the canyon-lands of northwest Texas or the San Juan Range in southwestern Colorado, wide open spaces call me to explore and discover, to make my life wider not narrower.

I need to see them often.

20

RETIREMENT IS A PLACE TOO

"We do not flourish as human beings when we belong to no place and no place cares about us."

— STEVEN GARBER

IF YOU DO an Internet search for retirement places, you will find most articles discussing geography. For instance, *U.S. News* has a list of the 25 best places to retire in the United States (all major metropolitan areas).[1] The researchers' criteria included things like affordability, taxes and healthcare, as well as intangibles like "happiness" and "desirability." The latter were determined by surveys, which, I assume, used a Likert scale to quantify people's feelings about their own place. (On a scale of 1 to 5 how happy are you living in Amarillo? Hmm. Is this a trick question?)

At the top of the list was Lancaster, Pennsylvania because, said the writers, the area is filled with Amish farmland and old warehouses that are being made into "hip restaurants and bars," which, I'm guessing, are not frequented by Amish farmers. Fort Myers, Florida came in at number two. The state had the most "best places," with seven of the top 25: In addition to Fort Meyers (2) were Sarasota (3), Lakeland (10), Daytona Beach (13), Miami (21), Melborne (23) and Jacksonville (24). My state of Texas came in at number two with Austin (4), San Antonio (8), Dallas-Fort Worth (9) and El Paso (11). Seriously? Washington D.C. was on the list (12), as was New York City (16), Phoenix (17) and Boston (25).

Yet, it seems that not all Americans want to retire in America. So *U.S. News* found the 10 best, affordable places to retire overseas.[2] For this analysis, researchers looked at things like cost of living and Real Estate prices, as well as healthcare, recreation, low crime rates and whether English was spoken there. First on this list was Algarve, Portugal, which has 3300 hours of sunshine a year (Yuma, Arizona has more, 4014 days; just sayin'). Portugal also has the number two spot, Cascais, which, in addition to cobblestone sidewalks, is "one of the world's most affordable places to embrace a luxury standard lifestyle on the ocean." France, also, made the list twice: Occitonie (6) where "everyday life is like something out of Disney's 'Beauty and the Beast'" (That's a good thing?) and Annecy (8) where residents feast on "tartiflette, a melted potato and bacon pie smothered in reblochon cheese" (they had me at "bacon").

Just how affordable are these places? Well, Cuenca, Ecuador also has the cobblestone streets of Cascais, but here "a couple could live comfortably on a budget of $1,000 per month." So if you're short on cash, forget my chapters on money and move to Ecuador.

However, call me old fashioned or maybe it's because I'm an English major, but the quality of place has to be measured by more than cost of living and days of sunlight. In his famous "Wilderness Letter," Wallace Stegner wrote of America's wilderness as a place that "formed character," was "good for spiritual health" and offered a "geography of hope."[3] According to Keith Basso in *Wisdom Sits in Places*, the Western Apaches had a similar view. These native Americans saw their land (places) as "a part of us as we are a part of them." Riding horses through their traditional tribal lands, one of them described the rough, barren country: "Not many cows but many good places. Try to hold on to them."[4]

Steven Garber lives in another world than the Western Apaches. He resides in Washington, DC, is an academic who rubs shoulders with politicians and world leaders and lectures on vocation and the common good. Yet his conclusion was much the same as the Indian on horseback.

These are the truest truths of the universe: We do not flourish as human beings when we know no one and no one knows us, we do not flourish as human beings when we belong to no place and no place cares about us.[5]

I didn't discover these authors until after we chose a place to retire, but now I realize that the truth of their words somehow found its way into our souls. Call it a serendipity, a calling, even a coincidence, but the feeling of hope was strong here. It was a good place, and we plan to hold on. By the way, surveys show that 80% of American retirees choose not to move at all.[6] A convenience? Maybe, or maybe people just know when they're already home.

PRAY FOR WILLIANCE

JUNE 17, 2016:

PLEASE PRAY for my friend Williance.

He is from Cameroon and married to Chrystelle, one of my all-time favorite students.

This young couple left their home country nearly five years ago—he to France and she to the U.S.—so they could one day make a successful life together.

Chrystelle flew to Paris in December of 2014 where they married. Last September, Williance joined her in Amarillo. I signed papers as his sponsor.

Ten days ago this sweet couple was blessed with their first child, a winsome little guy named James.

Yesterday, Williance was found unconscious in their apartment pool. Last night we almost lost him.

I'm convinced he's still alive because of the fervent prayers of an amazing wife, who refused to let him go, and who fought with the best weapon any of us could choose under similar circumstances.

Williance is stable, but we don't yet know the extent of his brain activity. Thus, my prayer request.

Some days, there are more important things to share than the musings of a retired English prof.

This is one of them.

21

UNWELCOME SURPRISES

"When pain is to be borne, a little courage helps more than much knowledge, a little human sympathy more than much courage, and the least tincture of the love of God more than all."

— C. S. Lewis

WILLANCE DIDN'T MAKE IT. He went too long without oxygen; it's that simple, but there's nothing simple about grief. What can I say? My heart was broken, grief multiplied by all the broken hearts of those I loved who loved Williance. His death, coming as it did just two weeks after I left Amarillo College, reminded me of those unwelcome surprises in life, a subject that needs addressed in any honest book on retirement.

In the 90s, I penned a newspaper column on what I called "the myth of normalcy." Quoting British writer Harry Blamires, I wrote, "Do we not feel it more natural for things to go right than for things to go wrong?" Blamires was lamenting the fact that many of his countrymen were looking forward to "a return to normalcy" after the end of World War II. After explaining that the end of the war would not (could not) bring a utopian normalcy to Britain, Blamires noted,

> There may not be a 'Law of Maximum Bloodiness,' but there is certainly no 'Law of Optimum Luck.' The 'state of emergency' does not end when war gives place to peace... Life is an ever-present emergency for all too many of our fellow-creatures.[1]

And, of course, many of these "fellow creatures" are retirees. I know. As I write these words, I have a good friend who is fighting stage 4 cancer; another friend is struggling with insurmountable debt; still another has lost her life partner and best friend. So how does one deal with hardships that come at a time in life when we are expecting the very opposite?

Frankly, not many retirement books address the subject. Nancy Schlossberg (*Revitalizing Retirement*) was an exception. "Unfortunately, not all surprises are positive. You may be happy leading your life when suddenly you encounter age discrimination on your job, you receive a diagnosis of a life-threatening illness, or someone close to you dies."[2] What can one do to prepare for such trauma? Schlossberg recommended having a Plan B.

I get that. I'm already on to Plan B for more income, and Plan C may not be far behind. Dr. Schlossberg quoted Bateson who called adult life "an improvisatory art,"[3] which sounded to me like I may have many plans before I'm done, some of which will need to be made up on the fly. But having a backup plan doesn't address the emotional toll exacted by such emergencies. What does? Here's where my research got personal. I asked—my hurting friends, that is.

One said she kept reviewing the "many times" God had carried her through other stormy times. Another suggested a bestselling book by Lysa Terkeurst (who is not a retiree but qualifies as a fellow sufferer who knows the terrain). Terkeurst's book, which, at the time of this writing, is ranked number one among Christian books on Amazon, is titled *It's Not Supposed to Be This Way*. I took a quick look (lots of good stuff here) and especially liked a quote in chapter seven where she draws a contrast between news (read "unwelcome surprises") and truth (God's Word): "News comes at us to tell us what we are dealing with. Truth comes from God and then helps us process all we are dealing with. News and truth aren't always one and the same."[4]

All of my interviewees mentioned the help of caring and faithful friends, the kind who don't give unsolicited or judgmental advice, who just show up (no avoiding) and listen, who let the sufferer set the agenda (what do you want to do/talk about today?). I made a mental note to surround myself with such people when life turns hard.

Finally, a woman I've admired for years (who has beaten cancer multiple times) told me that friends and family aren't enough. One has to take responsibility for her own recovery: "You have to be your own hero first as no one will win the battle if they aren't on the front line."

Words like these humble me. These are people "whose sandal straps I am unworthy to untie." C. S. Lewis captured my feelings in *The Problem of Pain*:

You would like to know how I behave when I am experiencing pain, not writing books about it. You need not guess, for I will tell you; I am a great coward.

When pain is to be borne, a little courage helps more than much knowledge, a little human sympathy more than much courage, and the least tincture of the love of God more than all.[5]

THE PROBLEM WITH GOLF

JULY 20, 2016

IN MY FIRST golf lesson in 50 years, I hit four beauties—they went straight, high and long and made Casey the golf pro smile (he was working wonders with this old man).

The problem is I hit a total of 50 balls. Twelve of them (triple the number of beauties) dribbled a few feet off the tee. One hit a goose (no, that's not a golfing term—a real goose).

And therein lies the problem with golf, and the reason I've tried to avoid it for most of my adult life.

If one manages to write a beautiful sentence, chances are another one is close behind. And more will follow. At least few will look like a first-grader wrote them.

Not so with golf.

"So what went wrong with that one"? I said to Casey
the golf pro.
"Your back swing was too close to your body."
"And that one?"
"Your back foot didn't pivot."
"What about that one?"

"You raised up. Keep your head down."

And so the conversation went. There are over 40 ways (seriously, I counted) one can mess up a golf swing.

And that, friends, is the problem with golf.

Yes, I'm going back. Sanity has never been a strong suit.

22

IT'S ONLY TOO LATE IF YOU DON'T
START NOW

"Quit today, and don't retire."

— STEPHEN POLLAN

THE MOST FREQUENT question I got during the first year was "How are you liking retirement?" followed closely by "Would you do it again?" I lied about the first (people didn't want to hear my whining), but I was blunt about the second. No, I would not retire. If I had it to do again, I would work another three to five years. Even at 67, I was at my best. The only problem was a decline in hearing, but hearing aids and compensatory teaching strategies could fix that. Such a decision would have no doubt been best financially. With the increases in equity in our rental properties and the bull market affecting my 401K, we were increasing net worth by about 8% per year. (For more reasons why working longer can be better, see Appendix A: The Joy of Working Longer.)

I felt deceived by my employer. I know my decision was voluntary, and the college was nice to offer a buy-out. But while we (the largest number of new retirees in the history of our institution) were provided countless meetings and counseling sessions on how to navigate the technical parts of leaving, no one offered counseling on the pitfalls. No one warned us of the psychological and financial turmoil we might face. So although I loved Amarillo College and always will, I warned those thinking about early retirement. "Your employer is not your friend," I would say. "Might as well face it; their concern is with their future, not yours." As it turned out, I was not alone in my assessment. Confirmation came in a book by Stephen Pollan, but I'm getting ahead of myself.

For now, know that many of the authors I was reading devoted a lot of copy to when one should pull the trigger, quit their jobs and "begin" retirement. Most of these were financial advisors and planners and most promoted the money-first concept of retirement planning. When I could generate 80 to 110 percent of preretirement income, or when I could amass savings equal to eight times my annual salary, I could quit my job.

But others questioned the strategy. Lee Eisenberg wrote a whole book about it. Entitled *The Number: What Do You Need for the Rest of Your Life, and What Will It Cost*, Eisenberg's book offered a wide range of opinions (from one to $15 million needed for a comfortable lifestyle). In the end, and after interviewing the likes of George Kinder, he decided there was no number:

> Money—the number—messes with your head and heart. Money—the number makes you stay in a job, live in a place you really don't like. Money—the Number—makes trouble between you and your spouse... Money—the Number— makes you feel empty... You live, travel, eat, and tee off at

the best. You'd think all this would make you happy, but it doesn't.[1]

Of course, the reason money, the Number, doesn't make one happy has been the thesis of this book. It takes a dream to be a successful, happy retiree and the money-first or money-only approach neglects that discussion. Besides, it was a moot point for me. I had retired before I really researched the pros and cons of my decision. Enter Stephen Pollan.

Pollan, author of *Die Broke: A Radical, Four-Part Financial Plan*, wrote, "Quit today, and don't retire."[2] I know the advice seems contradictory, but this is what he meant. In the new world in which we live, employers no longer take care of you in retirement. When they no longer need you or no longer can afford you, they're going to get rid of you (a buy-out if you're lucky). But the reality is you will not be better off after leaving (certainly not in the short run). The statistics are clear. Laid off, older workers are not covered up with job offers at or above (or even near) their former salaries.

So, wrote Pollan, "quit today: mentally separate yourself from your employer and realize that you're on your own. Abandon any remaining tinges of loyalty to your employer (who long ago abandoned any sense of obligation to you)."[3] Instead, Pollan wanted older employees to think of themselves the way free-agent athletes do. In the present, they should make the best deal they can, but they should always be looking for the next opportunity.

There's a twist to my story. Three years in, I have a different answer to the second question. If I could push rewind and choose again, yes, I would retire just when I did. Why? Steve the Economics prof would call it "opportunity cost." Opportunity cost is the value of what you could have chosen, of what you miss by choosing one thing over another.

If I had not retired when I did, I would not be in this house (not yet anyway), I would not have enjoyed the richest three years with family and friends we've ever experienced, and I couldn't have written this book or engaged in other gigs I would need to support retirement whenever it came. And there's another principle at work.

A recent survey showed that 60% of baby boomers fear running out of money in retirement.[4] But my research has suggested the alternative. Most of us will run out of time before we run out of money. The greatest advantage of retirement is you have more control over your greatest asset (time, not money). So, whether you stay at your career job or not, I'd take Pollan's advice and quit now. The title of Barbara Sher's book says it best: *It's Only Too Late If You Don't Start Now.*[5]

ON THRIVING

MAY 12, 2019

I WANT TO BE SAPPY. No, not that way.

Psalm 92:14 says those who walk with God can "still yield fruit in old age; they shall be full of sap and very green." That's the New American Standard version. The Message translation says "They'll grow tall in the presence of God, lithe and green, virile still in old age."

The Living Bible says "even in old age they will still produce fruit and be vital and green." And the Amplified version is the best: "They will still thrive and bear fruit and prosper in old age."

Thriving—I like that.

What I mean is, as I grow older, I don't want to settle.

You know, settle with a body that can no longer climb or bike. Settle with a mind that no longer learns new things. Settle with an income where we barely get by. Settle with a life that fails to touch others the way it once did. Most importantly, I don't want to settle with a spirit that no longer cares, that no longer dreams and strives.

In short, I want to be sappy.

23

EXCEPT YOU BECOME AS LITTLE CHILDREN

"We play because we want to and because it is fun."

— GEOFFREY GODBEY

I WAS APPROACHING the end of my research but still hadn't discovered one of the most important things I had looked forward to in the days preceding retirement. In a blog post, I called it "unstructured leisure, the kind children enjoy where they can plan their days spontaneously as they unfold." And so began a study of leisure and play and children.

According to Dora Costa (*The Evolution of Retirement, 1880-1990*), "increasing numbers of retirees are citing a preference for leisure as their main motivation for leaving the labor force,"[1] a trend that might have led Geoffrey Godbey to write, "At the end of your life, what you've done with your leisure may be more important than what you've done at work."[2]

Godbey is an expert in leisure. When I discovered him, he was Professor Emeritus of the Department of Park, Recreation and Tourism Management at Penn State University. Godbey had authored 100s of scholarly articles and 10 major books. I bought *The Evolution of Leisure* (1988) and *Leisure in Your Life: New Perspectives* (2008). The works were more academic than I was seeking, but I liked the prominence he gave the subject: "What you do during nonworking hours may determine your happiness, your contribution to the world, and even the meaning of your life as much as what you do in your occupational or obligated time."[3]

I also enjoyed Dr. Godbey's list of favorite leisure-time activities (expressed by percent). Following are some takeaways. In 2004, reading was the number one leisure activity for all U.S. adults (35%). Spending time with family/kids was second (21%). Others I found interesting were fishing (number five at eight percent, just behind going to movies at 10%), walking (number eight at six percent) and bicycling (near the top of my list, but number 26 for most people at three percent, which was just ahead of playing cards, an activity enjoyed by two percent of the populace).[4]

Godbey said the order changed somewhat for retiring baby boomers where traveling was number one, family was still second, fishing was still in the mix at number five, golfing was six, reading fell to eight (but was still significant: "Those over age 55 account for about one-third of book purchases") and exercise was nine ("People ages 55 and over are actually more likely to exercise than younger people").[5]

I found all of this thought provoking, but it wasn't what I was seeking. Godbey got closer when he wrote of "play," a concept he said was used interchangeably with leisure, but actually was different. Leisure is time-specific (non-work activities); play can be done at work or during free time. And there was another important difference. According to Godbey, play is "irrational, done for its own sake, and cannot be understood in purely rational, scientific terms (even though scholars keep trying). We play because we want to and because it is fun."[6]

Now, that's what I was looking for: how to play, or how to learn to play again. I don't think I need to explain my use of the preposition. All of us tend to associate play with what we did in childhood. We remember *playing* with friends. When parents told us to go outside and *play*, we knew what they meant. More importantly, we knew what we meant, what we would do, what playing was—for us.

By the way, in my search for play, I found I was not alone. There was a market for books on the subject. For instance, Stella Rheingold told me *101 Fun Things to Do in Retirement* (although I'm not particularly fond of jewelry making, scrapbooking or pottery). And Dorothy Cantor in *What Do You Want to Do When You Grow Up*, listed over a dozen criteria for what she called "serious leisure" (things like choosing something in your budget, something that can be practiced all year long and an activity that can be pursued in spite of physical limitations).[7] That's practical, I suppose, but what I wanted was not, or didn't have to be (practical, that is). I wanted what I had as a child, something spontaneous, maybe unexpected, and, most of all, fun.

Something closer to my hopes was a concept called "flow," introduced by psychologist Mihalyi Csikszentmihalyi and mentioned by both Godbey and Cantor. According to Csikszentmihalyi, one has "flow" with any activity "so gratifying that people are willing to do it for its own sake, with little concern for what they will get out of it, even when it is difficult, or dangerous."[8] Cantor said an activity with "flow" produces a "where did the time go" moment.[9] Godbey said that with flow one is "unselfconscious."[10]

I was getting closer. Research about play ultimately led me to Dr. Stuart Brown, who is to the study of play what

Godbey is to leisure. A medical doctor and psychiatrist, Brown was the founder of the National Institute for Play (sounds like a place I'd like to work). In his 2009 book *Play: How It Shapes the Brain, Opens the Imagination, and Invigorates the Soul*, Brown cited clinical studies of both people and animals.

Did you know that Labrador and wolf pups look alike? And, according to Brown, they act alike. They both have an "eagerness to play."[11] But when wolves reach adulthood, they become more serious about hunting and pack formation. Puppy play is rarely practiced. Labs, on the other hand, bring their juvenile characteristics into adulthood, something Dr. Brown called "neoteny" (the word means to stretch or extend). Brown said that Labs have an evolutionary advantage. Neoteny (caused by playfulness) allows them to be more open to change and sustained curiosity—which means they can learn and adapt to new challenges.[12]

The good news is humans, too, have neoteny. Wrote Brown, "Humans are the youthful primates. We are the Labradors of the primate world."[13] Translation: Retirees can play and need to play, or, to put it in the words of an "All Things Considered" segment on NPR: "Adults Need Recess Too."[14]

In a chapter called "We Are Built to Play," Brown said we have different play personalities. There's the joker (practices some kind of nonsense), the kinesthete (likes movement), the explorer, the competitor, the director (born organizers), the collector, the artist/creator and the storyteller (authors, play-wrights).[15] Dr. Brown also wanted me to discover my "play history." "Find that joy from the past and you are halfway to learning how to create it again in your present life."[16]

It was interesting that he mentioned the present. Zimbardo and Boyd had said we can look for happiness in the past or future, but we "experience happiness only in the present."[17] Their research showed that adults who live with a present time perspective are more playful and impulsive, are given to excitement and novelty and are spontaneous. They make friends easily and frequently and laugh significantly more than future and past oriented folks. The Stanford psychologists pointed out that all of us begin life as presents. Children don't look backward or forward but live in the now.

That's what I was looking for, what I'm still looking for, and I think I know where to find it. Stuart Brown made it clear: "As children, we don't need instruction in how to play. We just find what we enjoy and do it."[18]

So, instead of letting the experts tell me how to play, I thought I'd try a better way. "Except you become as little children," said Jesus. Of course, our Lord was talking about entering the Kingdom of Heaven, but I decided the same could apply to the kingdom of play. If I wanted to know how to play, I needed to learn from the boy who was I.

And I don't think he will be hard to find. I'm pretty sure he's been looking for me, too.

JOY SUSTAINED US

JANUARY 11, 2017

It's the best decision I've ever made.

Building a home on this little tributary canyon of the Palo Duro.

Because building a house, like going back to school or starting an encore career, is a vote for the future. Everything you do (from foundation work to framing to trim carpentry) anticipates a better tomorrow.

So building has been a hopeful metaphor. What first seemed impossible became possible, then doable, probable and, finally, done. It has given hope for other retirement goals.

But while hope is a strong thing, it's not what sustained us this year. The word is joy—hand-clapping, jumping-up-and-down joy. Sounds childish, huh?

It's felt childish. Since late August when we secretly slipped into our almost-finished home, we've felt like children on Christmas morning.

There were new presents to unwrap every day: visiting with friends on the front porch, chasing grandkids down steep hills, a different room/area to enjoy (you gotta see this fireplace) or all the opportunities to create (we've only begun landscaping—I'm planning a mountain stream in time for summer).

Let's be honest. Dave Ramsey would not be happy— building a new home at this time in our life was not the wisest business decision I've made. But I know this: My greatest stress has become my greatest joy.

And, in Ramsey's words, that's better than I deserve.

24

OLD MIKE'S PEAK

"It ain't over till it's over."

— Yogi Berra

It was my 70th summer before I was able to climb Wheeler again. The first year of retirement we had been busy building; the second, I couldn't find a hiking partner. So in July of 2018, when my friend Michael said he would join me, I was more than excited—and a bit apprehensive. Would the knees still hold? They did, and when we summited around 8:30 on a July morning, I told my fellow hiker the story of my first attempt on New Mexico's highest point.

In 2006, the 57-year-old version of me had taken a circuitous route up the mountain's east side where I met a young, married couple who had spent the night camping at Horseshoe Lake, maybe 600 vertical feet below Wheeler. They asked directions to the top. I told them I had never been there, but did have a Forest Service map. We looked at it together, trying to decide which peak was Wheeler, the one directly above us to the west or another to the southwest. My guess was the one to the southwest, which seemed more impressive to this novice, mountaineer wannabe.

I said I'd like to hike it with them but had already been nine miles and didn't think I had the energy to reach the top and still return to my pickup truck that day. They thanked me and proceeded to the peak, which I now know as Old Mike's Peak (Aptly named, don't you think? But definitely not Wheeler.) Old Mike's looked like what I thought peaks should look, a distinct hump at the end of a long narrow trail along a steep ridge with severe exposure (read "sheer drops of 1,000 feet or more") on both sides. On a windy day, Old Mike's would be dangerous, even for a walk-up. I'm glad it wasn't windy that day.

Since then, and in nearly 20 trips to my favorite peak, I've looked for that couple. I'd like to say I'm sorry.

And I'm glad I didn't do that to you, which certainly could have happened, if the neutral zone had not silenced me near the end of my first year of retirement. There are a number of topics I've not addressed in this book—things like long-term care, Medicare and health insurance, various types of retirement communities, retirement for singles (most of us will end up here for at least a little while), public policy (being unprepared for retirement is more than an individual problem)—the list goes on. But doing so would make this work too long, and, more importantly, would risk pointing you toward Old Mike's.

I'll be honest with you. Three years studying retirement does not make one an expert. However, three years living retirement can produce its own wisdom. So accept these words as those of a veteran, a fellow traveler, and, yes, fellow struggler, one who hasn't reached the peak yet, who has been lost on the mountain as much as not, yet one who is enjoying the climb, and the company, including you.

THIS OLD MAN IS DREAMING

JULY 12, 2016

Author's note: I guess I lied to you. The key to a happy retirement is not really a secret; is it? Your calling has been pursuing you all your life. You just have to recognize it, embrace it, turn it into dreams for retirement. And speaking of dreams, here is my final blog:

"YOUR OLD MEN WILL DREAM DREAMS," writes the prophet Joel (Joel 2:28d – NIV).

Of course, dreaming is not only for the old. Children dream—I once dreamed of riding a horse across my own Texas ranch. Adolescents dream—of a cute girl or handsome guy. My college students dreamed—of the successful life that would come as a result of their academic efforts.

So what is the significance of the old dreaming?

Maybe, it's because it's unexpected. Older people are supposed to be looking back on life; dreaming looks forward. Dreaming is not nostalgic but hopeful. A dreamer doesn't pine for what used to be, but envisions what can be, what will be.

Joel says the old dream when the Lord pours out his Spirit on all mankind.

Which must be happening now because this old man is dreaming.

Now available!

The Best Is Yet To Be Journal: Write your way to a creative, happy retirement.

"Dr. Bellah's companion Journal for *The Best is Yet to Be* is a great way to organize thoughts, to make note of all those retirement ideas, hopes, and dreams, and to pencil in plans that come to light in the process. I read the book a couple of times and had sticky notes and pieces of paper everywhere on which I jotted ideas and was working through some of the suggestions in the early chapters.

"The journal was just what I needed to get organized, think through some of the hard questions, and figure out how to be successful at retirement—the second time around! I especially like the Dream Pages, and I highly recommend using the journal as a companion to the book!"

— Carolyn

More details on the About the Author page

APPENDIX A

THE JOY OF WORKING LONGER

"But isn't that the point?" My friend was responding to my reply to her question. She wanted to know if I was enjoying retirement, and I answered that I didn't like the inactivity. "But isn't that the point?" In the conversation to follow, her assumption was that one works hard for 40 or 50 years so he or she doesn't have to work. The joy of retirement is not working. Really?

Lydia Bronte (*The Longevity Factor: The New Reality of Long Careers and How It Can Lead to Richer Lives*) would disagree with my friend. Her book, 25 years old now, presents a spirited defense for extended, working careers. In 1993, Dr. Bronte, who directed the Aging Society Project funded by the Carnegie Corporation, wanted to know about the outliers. For 40 years the percentages of those over 55 in the U.S. workforce had been declining (from 65% in 1950 to 38% in 1990).[1] But what about the outliers, those in the 38%? Bronte wanted to know what made them tick. She said she "was looking for patterns, something to explain why, why they stayed active and committed to working."[2]

So over a period of five years, Bronte interviewed 150 people who had continued working after age 65. Some were famous. Dr. Jonas Salk, inventor of the polio vaccine, was 79. Others were more ordinary. Elizabeth Burns, who described herself as "a good all-round office worker," was 89. There were 86 men and 64 women, all between the ages of 65 and 101. It was not a scientifically random sample but what my graduate school teachers would call a sample of convenience (Bronte found those who were available and willing to talk). Tellingly, all of the respondents said they continued to work by choice, not economic necessity, even though some found the extra income useful. "Wherever I went," wrote Bronte, "I found active older people, working at an enormous variety of pursuits in many different circumstances, apparently enjoying what they were doing."[3]

Over time, Bronte did find patterns. In the end, her interviewees fell into six categories:

Homesteaders

According to Bronte, homesteaders stayed in the same field but seemed "endlessly fascinated"[4] with what they were doing. Included in this group were artists, physicians, scientists and institution builders (of for-profit or nonprofit organizations).[5] The advantage to not retiring for a homesteader is obvious. Present success builds on past success. Who would want to walk away from that? My rancher, great, great grandfather, who lived to 86, was (fittingly) a homesteader.

Transformers

Bronte said that transformers had hit a bump in the road (probably at midlife) but came out with a new career and new passion, and, thus, didn't want to retire. From the transformers, Bronte said she learned "it is literally never too late to change and never too late to learn something new."[6] I realized that I, too, had been a transformer. My career as a college professor began when I had to change careers in my early 40s. I would add that we transformers find a lot of energy and passion with the second career, and we would not want to give that up easily. But I did give it up, way too easily it seems now. So if Bronte had interviewed me, I would say that some of us who would normally delay retirement can be induced to accepting it (peer pressure, monetary incentives—there are many reasons).

Late Bloomers

According to Bronte, Late Bloomers had careers that peaked later in life, and who would want to leave that? The success of these folks "continued to rise after ages when common wisdom assumes that people are winding down."[7] Bronte went on to say that some late bloomers started a new career later in life while some hit their peak in the old career late in life. What did she learn from the late bloomers? "The experience of these people demonstrates one thing over and over: growth and creativity are possible at any age, for all of us. What holds us back is the idea that growth stops."[8]

Explorers

With 40% of the Study's participants, the Explorers were the more numerous and the ones who changed careers more often, from three to 10 times.[9] They changed for a variety of reasons—unmet expectations, market opportunities, family considerations—and, being "extremely active."[10] Explorers "made the most radical career shifts," not only changing jobs, but whole fields.[11] Bronte thought that this group might be the best adapted for life in the 21st century. She was remarkably prescient (remember, she was writing in 1993):

> The Explorer, with his or her constantly expanding horizon, is a highly contemporary figure. The ability to adjust well to change may allow the individual to fill multiple roles at work, adapt quickly to rapidly evolving technology, and absorb the stresses and strains of recessions, plant closings, corporate downsizing, and early retirement.[12]

Retirers and Returners

Finally, Bronte wrote that Retirers and Returners retired to a life of leisure but went back to work "having missed the activity and challenges."[13] My friend Earl, who is 85, fit this pattern. Diagnosed with terminal cancer in his early 70s, he went home to die. Five years later, the carpet store he had managed asked him to come back. Today, he works half-days but is still their top salesperson. From returners like Earl, Bronte said she learned "retirement is another phase of life, not the end of it."[14]

Bronte made it clear that she was not against retirement: "There is nothing wrong with retirement for people who want or need to retire, and there is nothing wrong with the desire to continue working."[15] I needed to hear that second point. For some of us, richer lives are found not only in more satisfying leisure, but more meaningful and productive work. So, for now, I'm describing myself as a transformer who became a retirer, then returner, and now is trying to become a late bloomer in one of my gigs. Fingers crossed.

APPENDIX B

HOW C.S. LEWIS MADE ME LOVE HEAVEN

Note: The following words are taken from a talk I gave to a group in Amarillo called the C. S. Lewis Underground. They are important to this book because the message contributes significantly to the hope that is sustaining me in retirement. I realize not all readers share my Christian faith so I've included this segment as an appendix. Skip if you want. Or read on to see what one Christian thinks of the afterlife.

I have not always been a fan of Heaven. I like the idea of reunion, of seeing friends and family who have gone before me. And I cherish the thought of being face to face with Jesus. But I've never been a fan of Heaven's geography, at least not of the way it has been presented to me. Walking streets of gold or watching white robed people sit on puffy clouds while playing harps is not the way I want to spend eternity.

On a similar note, in his book *Heaven*, theologian Randy Alcorn wrote,

Sometimes when we look at the world's breathtaking beauty
—standing in a gorgeous place where the trees and flowers
and rivers and mountains are wondrous—we feel a twinge
of disappointment. Why? Because we know we're going to
leave this behind. In consolation or self-rebuke, we might
say. "This world is not my home." If we were honest,
however, we might add, "But part of me sure wishes it
was."[1]

I identify—or I did—until I read Lewis's *Last* Battle, the 7th
and final book in the Narnia series, which is to the *The Chronicles* as the Book of Revelation is to the Bible. It's Narnia's
apocalypse, the end of the world.

In the last chapter ("Further Up and Further In"), the children, who have died and gone to Narnia's Heaven, realize
that Aslan's Country looks much like the old Narnia, only
better. Speaking of the gorgeous mountains, Lucy says,
'"They're different. They have more colors on them and they
look further away than I remembered and they're more...
more...oh, I don't know..." "More like the real thing,"' said
Lord Digory softly.[2]

Then, the Lord Digory (the fictional professor who sounds
much like the story's author) goes on to explain Plato's
concept of seen and unseen reality. To Plato, the physical
universe was not ultimate reality but a copy or shadow of
something immaterial and invisible in the mind of God. The
old Narnia, Digory tells the children, '"was only a shadow or
copy of the real Narnia."' Then, he says this: '"You need not
mourn over Narnia, Lucy. All of the old Narnia that mattered,
all the dear creatures, have been drawn into the real Narnia...
and, of course, it is different; as different as a real thing is
from a shadow."'[3]

The story made me think about a trip to Europe several

years ago where I spent a half day alone hiking in the Swiss Alps above Lake Geneva. It is by far the most beautiful place I have visited. How I wished that what Lewis said about Narnia could be true about our world, that Heaven would be like this, but even better.

Well, Randy Alcorn says it is, that the promise God makes in Scripture is for a New Heaven *and New Earth*. And, he says, we have focused on the first but not the second, a practice that diminished my love for both. I should say that Alcorn is not some theological kook but a well-respected, biblical scholar. Rick Warren, pastor of the well-known Saddleback Community Church and author of *The Purpose Driven Life*, says Alcorn's book is the best he has read on Heaven. I thought it the longest book I had read on the subject. But Alcorn is a careful student of the text. His every argument is backed by extensive and relevant Scripture.

Thus, Alcorn's conclusion is stunning:

Everything changes when we grasp that all we love about the old Earth will be ours on the New Earth—either in the same form or another. Once we understand this, we won't regret leaving all the wonders of the world we've seen or mourn not having seen its countless other wonders. Why? Because we will yet be able to see them. God is no more done with the earth than he's done with us.[4]

Wow—not only will I someday get to hang out with Jesus but maybe we'll sit together in the Alps—places made new on the New Earth, more beautiful than one can imagine. It gets even better.

Alcorn said God, also, is not done with us. What does that mean? Well, the Bible says that on the New Earth we will receive resurrected, glorified bodies. In his collection of essays, *The Weight of Glory*, Lewis said this:

> It is a serious thing to live in a society of possible gods and goddesses, to remember that the dullest and most uninteresting person you can talk to may one day be a creature which, if you saw it now, you would be strongly tempted to worship.[5]

Similarly, Randy Alcorn says we need to "reform our vocabulary" about Heaven and the New Earth and New Bodies. He offers the following examples of phrases we use without thinking, but which, he says, are misleading, unscriptural and unhelpful.

- A preacher speaks of a Christian woman on the death of her Christian husband: "Little did she know that when she hugged her husband that morning, she would never hug him again."
- A man whose believing son had died, says, "That's the last time I'll ever see him in his body."
- Finally, a parent of a deceased daughter says, "I'll never see my daughter again on this earth."[6]

To these statements Alcorn responds,

> But in Heaven we won't be shadow people living in shadowlands... Instead we'll be fully alive and fully physical in a fully physical universe. In one sense, we've never seen our friend's body as truly as we will see it in the eternal Heaven. We've never been hugged here as meaningfully as we'll be hugged there. And we've never known this earth to be all that we will then know it to be.[7]

Back to Narnia and Lewis's idea of resurrected people who look and act like gods and goddesses—As the children move "further up and further in" towards Aslan's Country, they're in their new bodies but don't even realize it, except for what those bodies can do. The narrator says, "The country flew past as if they were seeing it from the windows of an express train. Faster and faster they raced, but no one got hot or tired or out of breath."[8]

Lewis writes, "if one could run without getting tired, I don't think one would often want to do anything else."[9] When the children come to Narnia's Great Waterfall, they all plunge in and start swimming directly for the cascading water. Lucy says, '"Have you noticed one can't feel afraid even if one wants to? Try it." "By Jove, one can't,"' said Eustace after he had tried.[10] And then they swim straight up the waterfall itself. "It was the sort of thing that would have been quite impossible in our world," writes Lewis—like climbing up light itself."[11]

So what gives hope beyond this life (read "retirement")? How about a place more beautiful and familiar than we ever imagined, experienced in bodies more strong and attractive than we ever dreamed? What's not to love about that?

NOTES

1. The History of American Retirement in Four Sketches

1. Costa, Dora L. *The Evolution of Retirement: An American Economic History, 1880-1990*. Chicago, IL: The University of Chicago Press, 1998.
2. "Gertrude Janeway, 93, Is Dead; Last Widow of a Union Soldier." Associated Press. The New York Times online. https://www.nytimes.com/2003/01/21/us/gertrude-janeway-93-is-dead-last-widow-of-a-union-soldier.html, January 21, 2003. Accessed October, 2018.
3. Mansfield, Duncan. "Civil War Romance Seems Like Only Yesterday to Soldier's Widow, 89." Associated Press. Online. http://articles.latimes.com/1998/sep/13/news/mn-22216, September 13, 1998. Accessed October, 2018.
4. Social Security History. Social Security website. https://www.ssa.gov/history/imf.html. Accessed October 2018.
5. Ibid., Accessed October, 2018.
6. Ring, Wilson. "Meet Ida May Fuller, Recipient of 1st Social Security Check 75 Years Ago." Associated Press. https://www.washingtontimes.com/news/2015/jan/30/ida-may-fuller-was-recipient-1st-social-security-c/. January 30, 2015. Accessed October 2018.
7. "A Place in the Sun." *Time*. August 3, 1962. http://content.time.com/time/magazine/article/0,9171,896472,00.html. Accessed October, 2018.
8. "Meades Getting Settled in New Sun City Arizona Community. *Mason City, Iowa, Globe-Gazette*, January 30, 1962, 14. Accessed October 2018.
9. Sun City Arizona History. http://suncityaz.org/discover/history/http://content.time.com/time/magazine/article/0,9171,896472,00.html [URL inactive]. Accessed October, 2018.
10. Ibid., Accessed October, 2018.
11. Stone, Howard, and Marika. *Too Young to Retire: 101 Ways to Start the Rest of Your Life*. New York, NY: The Penguin Group, 2002.
12. Ibid., 1.

2. Not Your Grandfather's Retirement

1. Dychtwald, Ken, Ph.D. *A New Purpose: Redefining Money, Family, Work, Retirement, and Success.* New York, NY: HarperCollins Publishers, 2009. 2.

2. Perls, Thomas T., M.D., and Margery Hutter Silver, Ed.D, with John F. Lauerman. *Living to 100: Lessons in Living to Your Maximum Potential at Any Age.* New York, NY: Basic Books, a member of the Perseus Books Group, 1999. 21.

3. Rowe, John W. M.D., and Robert L. Kahn, Ph.D. *Successful Aging: The Surprising Results of the MacArthur Foundation Study—the Most Extensive, Comprehensive Study on Aging in America.* New York, NY: Dell Publishing, 1998. 3.

4. Ibid., 5.

5. Ibid., 16.

6. Carstensen, Laura L., Ph.D. *A Long Bright Future: Happiness, Health, and Financial Security in an Age of Increased Longevity.* New York, NY: Broadway Books, an imprint of The Crown Publishing Group, a division of Random House, Inc., 2009. 5.

7. Life Expectancy Tables. DCC. https://www.cdc.gov/nchs/data/hus/2010/022.pdf. Accessed October 2018.

8. Freedman, Marc. *The Big Shift: Navigating the New State Beyond Midlife.* New York, NY: Public Affairs, a member of the Perseus Books Group, 2011. 50.

9. Carstensen, 1.

10. Freedman, 50.

11. Ibid.

12. Sheehy, Gail. *New Passages: Mapping Your Life Across Time.* New York, NY: A Ballantine Book, published by the Random House Publishing Group, 1995.

13. Lawrence-Lightfoot, Sara. *The Third Chapter: Passion, Risk, and Adventure in the 25 Years after 50.* New York, NY: Sarah Crichton Books, Farrar, Straus and Giroux, 2009.

14. Bateson, Mary Catherine. *Composing a Further Life: The Age of Active Wisdom.* New York, NY: Vintage Books, Random House, 2010.

15. Ibid., 24.

16. Freedman, 14.

17. Ibid., 13.

18. Pollan, Stephen M., and Mark Levine. *Die Broke: A Radical, Four-Part Financial Plan to Restore Your Confidence, Increase Your Net Worth, and Afford You the Lifestyle of Your Dreams.* New York, NY: HarperBusiness, a division of HarperCollins Publishers, 1997. 18.

19. Ibid., 52.

20. Anthony, Mitch. *The New Retirementality: Planning Your Life and Living Your Dreams...at Any Age You Want.* Hoboken, NJ: John Wiley & Sons, Inc., 2014. 36.

3. If You're Not Worried Yet, You Should Be

1. Ghilarducci, Teresa. *How to Retire with Enough Money: And How to Know What Enough Is.* New York: NY: Workman Publishing Co., Inc., 2015. 4, 23.
2. Social Security Benefits Planner: Retirement. http://www.ssa.gov. Accessed April 2019.
3. Ghilarducci, 11, 12.
4. Sarter, Michael. "Public Sector Jobs in States Where the Most People Work for the Government." Bureau of Labor Statistics. USA Today. https://www.usatoday.com/story/money/economy/2018/06/01/states-where-the-most-people-work-for-government/35302753/. Accessed June 1, 2018.
5. Reed, Eric. "What Are Average Retirement Savings in 2019?" The Street. https://www.thestreet.com/retirement/average-retirement-savings-14881067. March 3, 2019. Accessed April 2019.
6. Daily, Lyle. "You Won't Believe How Many Baby Boomers Have No Retirement Savings." The Motley Fool. https://www.fool.com/the-ascent/banks/articles/you-wont-believe-how-many-baby-boomers-have-no-retirement-savings/. January 25, 2019. Accessed April 2019.
7. Ghilarducci, 53.
8. Ibid., 52.
9. "How to Plan for Rising Health Care Costs." Fidelity. https://www.fidelity.com/viewpoints/personal-finance/plan-for-rising-health-care-costs. Accessed April 1, 2019.
10. Ghilarducci, 2.
11. Cabot, quoted in "A Place in the Sun." *Time.* August 3, 1962. http://content.time.com/time/magazine/article/0,9171,896472,00.html. Accessed October 2018.
12. Bridges, William. *Transitions: Making Sense of Life's Changes.* 2nd Edition. Cambridge, MA: Da Capo Press, a member of the Perseus Books Group, 2004. 17.

4. It Takes a Dream

1. Kinder, George, with Mary Rowland. *Life Planning for You: How to Design & Deliver the Life of Your Dreams.* Serenity Point Press, 2014. 43.

2. Stone, Howard, and Marika. *Too Young to Retire: 101 Ways to Start the Rest of Your Life*. New York, NY: The Penguin Group, 2002. 13.
3. Anthony, Mitch. *The New Retirementality: Planning Your Life and Living Your Dreams...at Any Age You Want*. Hoboken, NJ: John Wiley & Sons, Inc., 2014. 116.
4. Ibid., 14.
5. Ibid., 14.
6. Schlossberg, Nancy K. Ed.D. *Revitalizing Retirement: Reshaping Your Identity, Relationships, and Purpose*. Washington, DC: American Psychological Association, 2009. 20.
7. Bateson, Mary Catherine. *Composing a Further Life: The Age of Active Wisdom*. New York, NY: Vintage Books, Random House, 2010. 5.
8. Stone, 37.
9. Kinder, 91.
10. Ibid., 43-47.
11. Ibid., 93.
12. Ibid., 41.

5. Making Peace with the Past

1. Zimbardo, Philip, and John Boyd. *The Time Paradox: The New Psychology of Time That Will Change Your Life*. New York, NY: Free Press, a division of Simon & Schuster, Inc., 2008. 62.
2. Ibid., 62.
3. Ibid., 64.
4. Ibid., 86.
5. Wilson, Timothy D. Redirect: Changing the Stories We Live By. New York, NY: Back Bay Books / Little, Brown and Company, 2015.
6. Ibid., 4.
7. Ibid., 4.
8. Ibid., 9.
9. Ibid., 13.
10. Ibid., 51.
11. Zimbardo, 86.
12. Ibid., 93.

6. Who Am I

1. Guinness, Os. *The Call*. Nashville, TN: Thomas Nelson, 1998, 2003. 6.
2. Lawrence-Lightfoot, Sara. *The Third Chapter: Passion, Risk, and Adventure in the 25 Years after 50*. New York, NY: Sarah Crichton Books, Farrar, Straus and Giroux, 2009. 83.

3. Stone, Howard, and Marika. *Too Young to Retire: 101 Ways to Start the Rest of Your Life.* New York, NY: The Penguin Group, 2002. 8.
4. Schlossberg, Nancy K. Ed.D. *Revitalizing Retirement: Reshaping Your Identity, Relationships, and Purpose.* Washington, DC: American Psychological Association, 2009. 86.
5. Bateson, Mary Catherine. *Composing a Further Life: The Age of Active Wisdom.* New York, NY: Vintage Books, Random House, 2010.90.
6. Guinness,. 45.
7. Ibid., 16.
8. Ibid., 47.
9. Ibid., 44.

7. Dreamers of the Day

1. Leider, Richard J., and Alan M. Webber. *Life Reimagined: Discovering Your New Life Possibilities.* San Francisco, CA: Berrett-Koehler Publishers, Inc., 2013. 41.
2. Ibid., 120.
3. Quoted in Guinness, Os. *The Call.* Nashville, TN: Thomas Nelson, 1998, 2003. 175.
4. Stone, Howard, and Marika.*Too Young to Retire: 101 Ways to Start the Rest of Your Life.* New York, NY: The Penguin Group, 2002. 4.
5. Schlossberg, Nancy K., Ed.D. *Revitalizing Retirement: Reshaping Your Identity, Relationships, and Purpose.* Washington, DC: American Psychological Association, 2009. 86.
6. Kinder, George, with Mary Rowland. *Life Planning for You: How to Design & Deliver the Life of Your Dreams.* Serenity Point Press, 2014. 48-56.

8. Taking Inventory

1. Kinder, George, with Mary Rowland. *Life Planning for You: How to Design & Deliver the Life of Your Dreams.* Serenity Point Press, 2014. 144.

9. Budgeting 101

1. Hogan, Chris. *Retire Inspired: It's Not an Age; It's a Financial Number.* Brentwood, TN: Ramsey Press, The Lampo Group, Inc., 2016. 53.
2. Ghilarducci, Teresa. *How to Retire with Enough Money: And How to Know What Enough Is.* New York: NY: Workman Publishing Co., Inc., 2015. 34.

3. Jason, Julie. *The AARP Retirement Survival Guide: How to Make Smart Financial Decisions in Good Times and Bad.* New York, NY: AARP Books, an imprint of Sterling Publishing, 2009. 15.
4. Anthony, Mitch. *The New Retirementality: Planning Your Life and Living Your Dreams...at Any Age You Want.* Hoboken, NJ: John Wiley & Sons, Inc., 2014. 146.
5. Goodman, Miriam. *Reinventing Retirement: 389 Bright Ideas about Family, Friends, Health, What to Do, and Where to Live.* San Francisco, CA: Chronicle Books, 2008. 120.
6. Ramsey, Dave. "A Zero-Based Budget: What and Why." https://www.daveramsey.com/blog/zero-based-budget-what-why. Accessed October 2018.

10. Subtract before You Add

1. Anthony, Mitch. *The New Retirementality: Planning Your Life and Living Your Dreams...at Any Age You Want.* Hoboken, NJ: John Wiley & Sons, Inc., 2014. 1.
2. Stone, Howard, and Marika. *Too Young to Retire: 101 Ways to Start the Rest of Your Life.* New York, NY: The Penguin Group, 2002. 26.
3. Kinder, George, with Mary Rowland. *Life Planning for You: How to Design & Deliver the Life of Your Dreams.* Serenity Point Press, 2014. 136.
4. Ghilarducci, Teresa. *How to Retire with Enough Money: And How to Know What Enough Is.* New York: NY: Workman Publishing Co., Inc., 2015.63.
5. Ibid., 67.
6. Kinder, 107-108.
7. Ghilarducci, 66, 67.

11. Coon Skin Caps and Hula-Hoops

1. Strauss, Karsten. "Marc Freedman: Helping Others Find Passion, Purpose and a Paycheck with an Encore." Forbes. https://www.forbes.com/sites/karstenstrauss/2015/08/24/marc-freedman-helping-others-find-passion-purpose-and-a-paycheck-with-an-encore/#4ca7f63f2712. August 24, 2015. Accessed October, 2018.
2. Hannon, Kerry. AARP. "Great Jobs for Workers over 50." https://www.aarp.org/work/working-after-retirement/info-2015/great-jobs-for-50-plus-photo.html#slide1. Accessed April, 2019.
3. Stone, Howard, and Marika. *Too Young to Retire: 101 Ways to Start the Rest of Your Life.* New York, NY: The Penguin Group, 2002. 73.

4. Miller, Mark. *The Hard Times Guide to Retirement Security: Practical Strategies for Money, Work, and Living.* Hoboken, NJ: John Wiley & Sons, Inc., 2010. 146.

5. Phipps, Melissa. *The Retirement Rescue Plan: Retirement Planning Solutions for the Millions of Americans Who Haven't Saved Enough.* Berkeley, CA: Sonoma Press, 2016. 122.

6. Ibid., 125.

7. Ibid., 125.

8. Bellah, Mike. *Baby Boom Believers.* Wheaton, Ill: Tyndale House Publishers, 1988. 19.

9. Furlong, Mary S. *Turning Silver into Gold: How to Profit in the New Boomer Marketplace.* Upper Saddle River, NJ: FT Press, 2007. 4.

10. Ibid., 235.

12. Investing for Dummies

1. Jason, Julie. *The AARP Retirement Survival Guide: How to Make Smart Financial Decisions in Good Times and Bad.* New York, NY: AARP Books, an imprint of Sterling Publishing, 2009.

2. Solin, Daniel R. *The Smartest Retirement Book You'll Ever Read.* New York, NY: A Perigee Book, the Penguin Group, 2009.

3. Ghilarducci, Teresa. *How to Retire with Enough Money: And How to Know What Enough Is.* New York: NY: Workman Publishing Co., Inc., 2015.

4. Beckham, Steven. Personal interview, September 15, 2018.

5. Ghilarducci. 87.

6. Hogan, Chris. *Retire Inspired: It's Not an Age; It's a Financial Number.* Brentwood, TN: Ramsey Press, The Lampo Group, Inc., 2016. 46.

7. Solin. 33.

8. Ghilarducci. 76.

9. Ibid., 92.

10. "Money Scams and Fraud." AARP. https://www.aarp.org/money/scams-fraud/. Accessed April, 2019.

11. Kinder, George, with Mary Rowland. *Life Planning for You: How to Design & Deliver the Life of Your Dreams.* Serenity Point Press, 2014. 179-185.

12. Solin, 196-199.

13. Jason, 279-286.

13. They're Helping My Dreams Come True

1. Goodman, Miriam. *Reinventing Retirement: 389 Bright Ideas about Family, Friends, Health, What to Do, and Where to Live*. San Francisco, CA: Chronicle Books, 2008. 59.
2. Rowe, John W. M.D., and Robert L. Kahn, Ph.D. *Successful Aging: The Surprising Results of the MacArthur Foundation Study—the Most Extensive, Comprehensive Study on Aging in America*. New York, NY: Dell Publishing, 1998. 156.
3. Ornish, Dean, M.D. *Love & Survival: 8 Pathways to Intimacy and Health*. New York, NY: HarperCollins Publishers, 1998.
4. Ornish, qtd. in "Love and Survival." Harper Collins online. https://www.harpercollins.com/9780060930202/love-and-survival/. Accessed April, 2019.
5. Carstensen, Laura L., Ph.D. *A Long Bright Future: Happiness, Health, and Financial Security in an Age of Increased Longevity*. New York, NY: Broadway Books, an imprint of The Crown Publishing Group, a division of Random House, Inc., 2009. 97.
6. Leider, Richard J., and Alan M. Webber. *Life Reimagined: Discovering Your New Life Possibilities*. San Francisco, CA: Berrett-Koehler Publishers, Inc., 2013. 67.
7. Ibid., 68.
8. "You Can't Make Old Friends." Wikipedia. https://en.wikipedia.org/wiki/You_Can%27t_Make_Old_Friends. Accessed Octoberr, 2018.
9. Leider, 73-75.

14. Too Much of Him

1. Goodman, Miriam. *Too Much Togetherness: Surviving Retirement as a Couple*. Springville, Utah: Bonneville Books, an imprint of Cedar Fort, Inc., 2011. 17.
2. Ibid., xi.
3. Taylor, Roberta K. and Dorian Mintzer. *The Couple's Retirement Puzzle: 10 Must-Have Conversations for Creating an Amazing New Life Together*. Naperville, IL: Sourcebooks, Inc., 2014. xxxiii.
4. Ibid., xl.
5. Ibid., xli.
6. Ibid.,xxxix.
7. Ibid.,xl.
8. Ibid., xli.
9. Goodman, 33.

10. Lewis, C. S. *The Four Loves*. New York: Harcourt Brace Jovanovich Publishers, 1960, 61.
11. Goodman., 16.
12. Ibid., 65.
13. Sterk, Mary CFP. *Ready to Pull the Retirement Trigger*. New York, NY: Morgan James Publishing, 2017. 126.

15. Arctic Tundra, Spanish Skirts and Buffalo Grass

1. Rowe, John W. M.D., and Robert L. Kahn, Ph.D. *Successful Aging: The Surprising Results of the MacArthur Foundation Study—the Most Extensive, Comprehensive Study on Aging in America*. New York, NY: Dell Publishing, 1998. 66.
2. Ibid., 22.
3. Ibid., 23.
4. Ibid., 24.
5. Ibid., 24.
6. Ibid., 25.
7. Ibid., 97.
8. Ibid., 98.
9. Ibid., 104.
10. Crowley, Chris, and Henry S. Lodge, M.D. *Younger Next Year: Live Strong, Fit and Sexy—Until You're 80 and Beyond*. New York, NY: Workman Publishing, 2004.
11. Ibid., 103.
12. Ibid., 5.
13. Chen, Michael A., MD. "Being Active When You Have Heart Disease." https://medlineplus.gov/ency/patientinstructions/000094.htm. Accessed April 2019.
14. Mayo Clinic Staff. "Exercise: A Drug-Free Approach to Lowering High Blood Pressure." https://www.mayoclinic.org/diseases-conditions/high-blood-pressure/in-depth/high-blood-pressure/art-20045206. Accessed April 2019.
15. American Cancer Society. "Physical Activity and the Cancer Patient." https://www.cancer.org/treatment/survivorship-during-and-after-treatment/staying-active/physical-activity-and-the-cancer-patient.html. Accessed April 2019.

16. We Just Know Stuff

1. Rowe, John W. M.D., and Robert L. Kahn, Ph.D. *Successful Aging: The Surprising Results of the MacArthur Foundation Study—the Most Extensive, Comprehensive Study on Aging in America.* New York, NY: Dell Publishing, 1998. 126.
2. Ibid., 131.
3. Burke, quoted in Strauch, Barbara. *The Secret Life of the Grown-up Brain: The Surprising Talents of the Middle-Aged Mind.* Penguin Books, 2010. 70.
4. Ibid., 70.
5. Strauch, Barbara. *The Secret Life of the Grown-up Brain: The Surprising Talents of the Middle-Aged Mind.* Penguin Books, 2010.
6. Ibid., 16.
7. Ibid., xii.
8. Ibid.,47.
9. Ibid., xvi.
10. Rowe, 133.
11. Ibid., 134.
12. Strauch, 118.
13. Ibid., 59.
14. Ibid., 116, 174, 184.
15. Ibid., 91.
16. Ibid., 42.
17. Rowe, 133.
18. Lawrence-Lightfoot, Sara. *The Third Chapter: Passion, Risk, and Adventure in the 25 Years after 50.* New York, NY: Sarah Crichton Books, Farrar, Straus and Giroux, 2009. 243.
19. Rowan, Lisa. "Senior Citizens Can Go to College for Free or Cheap in All 50 States." The Pennyhoarder. November 2, 2016. https://www.thepennyhoarder.com/life/college/free-college-courses-for-senior-citizens/. Accessed October 2018.
20. Road Scholar Lifelong Learning Institute. https://www.roadscholar.org/about/lifelong-learning-institutes/ [URL inactive]. Accessed October 2018.
21. Osher Lifelong Learning Institutes (OLLI). The Bernard Osher Foundation. http://www.osherfoundation.org/index.php?olli. Accessed October 2018.

17. Hope Works

1. Rowe, John W. M.D., and Robert L. Kahn, Ph.D. *Successful Aging: The Surprising Results of the MacArthur Foundation Study—the Most Extensive,*

Comprehensive Study on Aging in America. New York, NY: Dell Publishing, 1998. 20.

2. Ibid., 134.
3. Strauch, Barbara. *The Secret Life of the Grown-up Brain: The Surprising Talents of the Middle-Aged Mind.* Penguin Books, 2010. 29.
4. Qtd. in Strauch. 31.
5. Qtd. in Strauch. 38.
6. Bellah, Mike. "The Expectation Effect." http://www.bestyears.com/expectations.html. Accessed October 2018.
7. Emmons, Robert. "Why Gratitude Is Good." https://greatergood.berkeley [URL inactive]. Edu/article/item/why_gratitude_is_-good. Accessed October 2018.
8. Ibid.,
9. Ibid.,
10. Kaufman, Scott Barry. "The Will and Ways of Hope: Hope Involves the Will to Get There, and Different Ways to Get There." Psychology Today. https://www.psychologytoday.com/us/blog/beautiful-minds/201112/the-will-and-ways-hope [URL inactive]. December 26, 2011. Accessed October 2018.
11. Snyder, C. R., et. al. "The Adult Trait Hope Scale 1991." Positive Psychology Tests and Measures. https://booksite.elsevier.com/9780123745170/Chapter%203/Chapter_3_Worksheet_3.4.pdf. Accessed October 2018.
12. Vine, W. E. *An Expository Dictionary of New Testament Words.* Old Tappan, NJ: Fleming H. Revell. 1952. 232.

18. Something from Nothing

1. Vaillant, George E., M.D. *Aging Well.* New York, NY: Little, Brown and Company, 2002. 240.
2. Ibid., 238.
3. Osler, qtd. in Bronte, Lydia, Ph.D. *The Longevity Factor: The New Reality of Long Careers and How It Can Lead to Richer Lives.* New York, NY: Harper Collins, 1993.
4. Ibid., 40.
5. Ibid., 41.
6. Ibid., 41.
7. Simonton, qtd. in Bronte, Lydia, Ph.D. *The Longevity Factor: The New Reality of Long Careers and How It Can Lead to Richer Lives.* New York, NY: Harper Collins, 1993. 49.
8. Ibid., 50.
9. Vaillant, 230.

10. Cameron, Julia. *It's Never Too Late to Begin Again: Discovering Creativity and Meaning at Midlife and Beyond.* New York, NY: A TarcherPerigee Book, an imprint of Penguin Random House, 2016. 322.
11. Ibid., xviii.
12. Ibid., 5.
13. Ibid., 74.
14. Ibid., 35.
15. Ibid., 110.

19. Becoming Dangerous Men and Women

1. Sterk, Mary CFP. *Ready to Pull the Retirement Trigger.* New York, NY: Morgan James Publishing, 2017. 5.
2. Cameron, Julia. *It's Never Too Late to Begin Again: Discovering Creativity and Meaning at Midlife and Beyond.* New York, NY: A TarcherPerigee Book, an imprint of Penguin Random House, 2016. 73.
3. Newhouse, Meg Ph.D. *Legacies of the Heart: Living a Life that Matters.* Columbia, SC: Ebook Bakery Books, 2016. 3.
4. Jones, Jeffrey M. "Majority in U.S. Do Not Have a Will." Gallup. https://news.gallup.com/poll/191651/majority-not.aspx. May 8, 2016. Accessed October 2018.
5. Ashford, Kate. "Horror Stories: When You Die Without A Will." *Forbes.* https://www.forbes.com/sites/kateashford/2016/06/30/no-will/#2a431a982f20. June 30, 2016. Accessed October 2018.
6. Erickson, qtd. in Vaillant, George E., M.D. *Aging Well.* New York, NY: Little, Brown and Company, 2002. 48.
7. Vaillant, George E., M.D. *Aging Well.* New York, NY: Little, Brown and Company, 2002. 132.
8. Newhouse, 183.
9. Vaillant, 48.
10. Newhouse, 247.
11. Byock, Ira, M.D. *The Four Things That Matter: A Book About Living.* New York, NY: Atria Books, A Division of Simon & Schuster, Inc. 2014. xi.
12. Newhouse, 58.
13. Alfred Lord Tennyson. "Ulysses." 1833.

20. Retirement Is a Place Too

1. Brandon, Emily. "The Best Places to Retire in 2019." U.S. News and World Report. https://money.usnews.com/money/retirement/slideshows/the-best-places-to-retire. October 10, 2018.

2. Peddicord, Kathleen. "The 10 Best Affordable Places to Retire Overseas in 2019." U.S. News and World Report. https://money.usnews.com/money/retirement/baby-boomers/slideshows/the-best-affordable-places-to-retire-overseas. December 17, 2018.

3. Stegner, Wallace. "Wilderness Letter." December 3, 1960. http://wilderness.org/content/wilderness-letter [URL inactive]. Accessed October 2018.

4. Basso, Keith H. Wisdom *Sits in Places: Landscape and Language among the Western Apache.* Albuquerque, NM: University of New Mexico Press, 1996. Xvi.

5. Garber, Steven. *Visions of Vocation: Common Grace for the Common Good.* Downers Grove, IL: Intervarsity Press. 2014. 133.

6. Taylor, Roberta K., and Dorian Mintzer. *The Couple's Retirement Puzzle: 10 Must-Have Conversations for Creating an Amazing New Life Together.* Naperville, IL: Sourcebooks, Inc., 2014. 196.

21. Unwelcome Surprises

1. Bellah, Mike. "The Myth of Normalcy." Our Best Years. http://www.bestyears.com/normal.html. Accessed October 2018.

2. Schlossberg, Nancy K., Ed.D. *Revitalizing Retirement: Reshaping Your Identity, Relationships, and Purpose.* Washington, DC: American Psychological Association, 2009. 194.

3. Bateson, qtd. in Schlossberg, 193.

4. Terkeurst, Lysa. *It's Not Supposed to Be This Way.* Nashville, TN: Nelson Books, an imprint of Thomas Nelson, 2018. 121.

5. Lewis, C. S. *The Problem of Pain.* New York, NY: Macmillan Publishing Co., Inc., 1962. 105, 10.

22. It's Only Too Late If You Don't Start Now

1. Eisenberg, Lee. *The Number: What Do You Need for the Rest of Your Life, and What Will It Cost?* New York, NY: Free Press, a division of Simon & Schuster, Inc., 2006. 214-15.

2. Pollan, Stephen M., and Mark Levine. *Die Broke: A Radical, Four-Part Financial Plan to Restore Your Confidence, Increase Your Net Worth, and Afford You the Lifestyle of Your Dreams.* New York, NY: HarperBusiness, a division of HarperCollins Publishers, 1997. 11.

3. Ibid., 11.

4. Sterk, Mary. *Ready to Pull the Retirement Trigger?* New York, NY: Morgan James Publishing. 2017.

5. Sher, Barbara. *It's Only Too Late If You Don't Start Now: How to Create Your Second Life at Any Age*. New York, NY: Dell Publishing, a division of Random House, Inc., 1998.

23. Except You Become As Little Children

1. Costa, Dora L. *The Evolution of Retirement: An American Economic History, 1880-1990*. Chicago, IL: The University of Chicago Press, 1998. 133.
2. Godbey, Geoffrey. *Leisure in Your Life: New Perspectives*. State College, PA: Venture Publishing, Inc., 2008. 1.
3. Ibid., 1.
4. Ibid., 12.
5. Ibid., 228.
6. Ibid.,
7. Cantor, Dorothy, with Andrea Thompson. *What Do You Want to Do When You Grow Up? Starting the Next Chapter of Your Life*. Boston, MA: Little, Brown and Company, 2000.
8. Qtd. in Cantor. 22.
9. Cantor, 59.
10. Godbey, 5.
11. Brown, Stuart, M.D. with Christopher Vaughan. *Play: How It Shapes the Brain, Opens the Imagination, and Invigorates the Soul*. New York, NY: The Penguin Group, 2010.
12. Ibid., 55.
13. Ibid., 55.
14. Yenigun, Sami. "Play Doesn't End with Childhood: Why Adults Need Recess Too." National Public Radio. All Things Considered. https://www.npr.org/sections/ed/2014/08/06/336360521/play-doesnt-end-with-childhood-why-adults-need-recess-too. Accessed April 2019.
15. Brown, 67.
16. Ibid., 206.
17. Zimbardo, Philip, and John Boyd. *The Time Paradox: The New Psychology of Time That Will Change Your Life*. New York, NY: Free Press, a division of Simon & Schuster, Inc., 2008. 10.
18. Brown, 6.

Appendix A

1. Bronte, Lydia, Ph.D. *The Longevity Factor: The New Reality of Long Careers and How It Can Lead to Richer Lives*. New York, NY: Harper Collins, 1993. 73.
2. Ibid., 83.

3. Ibid., 74.
4. Ibid., 100.
5. Ibid., 102.
6. Ibid., 154.
7. Ibid., 209.
8. Ibid., 237.
9. Ibid., 155.
10. Ibid., 156.
11. Ibid., 156.
12. Ibid., 180.
13. Ibid., 238.
14. Ibid., 238.
15. Ibid., 315.

Appendix B

1. Alcorn, Randy. *Heaven*. Carol Stream, IL: Tyndale House Publishers, Inc, 2004. 159.
2. Lewis, C. S. *The Last Battle*. New York: Collier Books--Macmillan Publishing Co., 1956. 168-169.
3. Ibid., 169.
4. Alcorn, 248.
5. Lewis, C. S. *The Weight of Glory and Other Addresses*. New York: Collier Books-- Macmillan Publishing Co., 1975. 18.
6. Alcorn. 136.
7. Ibid., 137.
8. Lewis. *Last Battle*, 171.
9. Ibid., 172.
10. Ibid., 173.
11. Ibid., 174.

SOURCES: BOOKS

Author's note: What I have done for much of this book is what English teachers call a "literature review;" that is, I have tried to give you a brief overview of the relevant works on retirement and its related topics. I've given you movie trailers, not the whole movie. I hope you will read many of these titles for yourself (believe me, there's a lot more there). The information that is getting me through retirement came from many sources, and reading each helped me find the others. I expect the same will be true for you.

Alcorn, Randy. *Heaven*. Carol Stream, IL: Tyndale House Publishers, Inc, 2004.

Anthony, Mitch. *The New Retirementality: Planning Your Life and Living Your Dreams...at Any Age You Want*. Hoboken, NJ: John Wiley & Sons, Inc., 2014.

Basso, Keith H. *Wisdom Sits in Places: Landscape and Language among the Western Apache*.

Albuquerque, NM: University of New Mexico Press, 1996.

Bateson, Mary Catherine. *Composing a Further Life: The Age of Active Wisdom*. New York, NY: Vintage Books, Random House, 2010.

Bellah, Mike. *Baby Boom Believers*. Wheaton, Ill: Tyndale House Publishers, 1988.

Birken, Emily Guy. *The 5 Years before You Retire*. Avon, MA: Adams Media, an imprint of Simon & Schuster, Inc., 2014.

Bratter, Bernice, and Helen Dennis. *Project Renewment: The First Retirement Model for Career Women*. New York, NY: Scribner, a division of Simon & Schuster, Inc., 2008.

Breus, Michael, Ph.D. *The Power of When: Discover Your Chronotype—and the Best Time to Eat Lunch, Ask for a Raise, Have Sex, Write a Novel, Take Your Meds, and More*. New York, NY: Little, Brown and Company, 2016.

Bridges, William. *Transitions: Making Sense of Life's Changes*, 2nd Edition. Cambridge, MA: Da Capo Press, a member of the Perseus Books Group, 2004.

Bronte, Lydia, Ph.D. *The Longevity Factor: The New Reality of Long Careers and How It Can Lead to Richer Lives*. New York, NY: Harper Collins, 1993.

Brown, Stuart, M.D. with Christopher Vaughan. *Play: How It Shapes the Brain, Opens the Imagination, and Invigorates the Soul*. New York, NY: The Penguin Group, 2010.

Byock, Ira, M.D. *The Four Things That Matter: A Book About Living*. New York, NY: Atria

Books, A Division of Simon & Schuster, Inc. 2014.

Cameron, Julia. *It's Never Too Late to Begin Again: Discovering Creativity and Meaning at Midlife and Beyond.* New York, NY: A TarcherPerigee Book, an imprint of Penguin Random House, 2016.

Cantor, Dorothy with Andrea Thompson. *What Do You Want to Do When You Grow Up? Starting the Next Chapter of Your Life.* Boston, MA: Little, Brown and Company, 2000.

Carstensen, Laura L., Ph.D. *A Long Bright Future: Happiness, Health, and Financial Security in an Age of Increased Longevity.* New York, NY: Broadway Books, an imprint of The Crown Publishing Group, a division of Random House, Inc., 2009.

Costa, Dora L. *The Evolution of Retirement: An American Economic History, 1880-1990.* Chicago, IL: The University of Chicago Press, 1998.

Crowley, Chris, and Henry S. Lodge, M.D. *Younger Next Year: Live Strong, Fit and Sexy— Until You're 80 and Beyond.* New York, NY: Workman Publishing, 2004.

Crowley, Chris, and Henry S. Lodge, M.D. *Younger Next Year for Women: Live Strong, Fit and Sexy—Until You're 80 and Beyond.* New York, NY: Workman Publishing, 2007.

Davis, Donna. *The New Retirement Basics: The Quick and Easy Guide to Social Security and Medicare.* Snowmass Village, CO: Golden Goddess Press, 2016.

Delaney, Brian M., and Lisa Walford. *The Longevity Diet: The Only Proven Way to Slow the Aging Process and Maintain Peak Vitality — Through Calorie Restriction.* Philadelphia, PA: Da Capo Press, a member of the Perseus Books Group, 2010.

Dychtwald, Ken, Ph.D. Age Power: *How the 21ˢᵗ Century Will Be Ruled by the New Old.* New York: NY: Jeremy P. Tarcher/Putnam, a member of Penguin Putnam Inc., 1999.

Dychtwald, Ken, Ph.D. *A New Purpose: Redefining Money, Family, Work, Retirement, and Success.* New York, NY: HarperCollins Publishers, 2009.

Emmons, Robert A., Ph.D. *Thanks!: How the New Science of Gratitude Can Make You Happier.* New York, NY: Houghton Mifflin Company, 2007.

Eisenberg, Lee. *The Number: What Do You Need for the Rest of Your Life, and What Will It Cost?* New York, NY: Free Press, a division of Simon & Schuster, Inc., 2006.

Freedman, Marc. *The Big Shift: Navigating the New State Beyond Midlife.* New York, NY: Public Affairs, a member of the Perseus Books Group, 2011.

Freedman, Marc. *Encore: Finding Work that Matters in the Second Half of Life.* New York, NY: Public Affairs, a member of the Perseus Books Group, 2007.

Freedman, Marc. *Prime Time: How Baby Boomers Will Revolutionize Retirement and Transform*

America. New York, NY: Public Affairs, a member of the Perseus Books Group, 1999.

Furlong, Mary S. *Turning Silver into Gold: How to Profit in the New Boomer Marketplace*. Upper Saddle River, NJ: FT Press, 2007.

Garber, Steven. *Visions of Vocation: Common Grace for the Common Good*. Downers Grove, IL: Intervarsity Press. 2014.

Geber, Sara Zeff, Ph.D. *Essential Retirement Planning for Solo Agers: A Retirement and Aging Roadmap for Single and Childless Adults*. Coral Gables, FL: Mango Publishing, 2018.

Ghilarducci, Teresa. *How to Retire with Enough Money: And How to Know What Enough Is*. New York: NY: Workman Publishing Co., Inc., 2015.

Godbey, Geoffrey. *Leisure in Your Life: New Perspectives*. State College, PA: Venture Publishing, Inc., 2008.

Goodman, Miriam. *Reinventing Retirement: 389 Bright Ideas about Family, Friends, Health, What to Do, and Where to Live*. San Francisco, CA: Chronicle Books, 2008.

Goodman, Miriam. *Too Much Togetherness: Surviving Retirement as a Couple*. Springville, Utah: Bonneville Books, an imprint of Cedar Fort, Inc., 2011.

Griffiths, Bob. *Do What You Love for the Rest of Your Life: A Practical Guide to Career Change and Personal Renewal*. New York, NY: Ballantine Books, 2001.

Guinness, Os. *The Call*. Nashville, TN: Thomas Nelson, 1998, 2003.

Hannon, Kerry. *Great Jobs for Everyone 50+.* Hoboken, NJ: John Wiley & Sons, Inc., 2018.

Heilbrun, Carolyn G. *The Last Gift of Time: Life Beyond Sixty.* New York, NY: Ballantine Books, 1997.

Hinden, Stan. *How to Retire Happy: The 12 Most Important Decisions You Must Make before You Retire.* New York, NY: McGraw-Hill, 2013.

Hogan, Chris. *Retire Inspired: It's Not an Age; It's a Financial Number.* Brentwood, TN: Ramsey Press, The Lampo Group, Inc., 2016.

Jacoby, Susan. *Never Say Die: The Myth and Marketing of the New Old Age.* New York: NY: Vintage Books, a division of Random House, Inc., 2011.

Jason, Julie. *The AARP Retirement Survival Guide: How to Make Smart Financial Decisions in Good Times and Bad.* New York, NY: AARP Books, an imprint of Sterling Publishing, 2009.

Kinder, George, with Mary Rowland. *Life Planning for You: How to Design & Deliver the Life of Your Dreams.* Serenity Point Press, 2014.

Kinder, George. *Seven Stages of Money Maturity: Understanding the Spirit and Value of Money in Your Life.* New York, NY: Dell Publishing, a division of Random House, Inc., 1999.

Koff, Art. *Invent Your Retirement: Resources for the Good Life.* Winchester, Virginia: Oakhill Press, 2006.

Laslett, Peter. *A Fresh Map of Life: The Emergence of the Third Age.* Cambridge, MA: Harvard University Press, 1989.

Lawrence-Lightfoot, Sara. *The Third Chapter: Passion, Risk, and Adventure in the 25 Years after 50*. New York, NY: Sarah Crichton Books, Farrar, Straus and Giroux, 2009.

Leider, Richard J., and Alan M. Webber. *Life Reimagined: Discovering Your New Life Possibilities*. San Francisco, CA: Berrett-Koehler Publishers, Inc., 2013.

Lewis, C. S. *The Four Loves*. New York: Harcourt Brace Jovanovich Publishers, 1960.

Lewis, C. S. *The Last Battle*. New York: Collier Books--Macmillan Publishing Co., 1956.

Lewis, C. S. *The Problem of Pain*. New York, NY: Macmillan Publishing Co., Inc., 1962.

Lewis, C. S. *The Weight of Glory and Other Addresses*. New York: Collier Books--Macmillan Publishing Co., 1975.

Malkiel, Burton G. *A Random Walk Down Wall Street: The Time-Tested Strategy for Successful Investing*. New York, NY. W. W. Norton & Company, Inc., 2015

Miller, Mark. *The Hard Times Guide to Retirement Security: Practical Strategies for Money, Work, and Living*. Hoboken, NJ: John Wiley & Sons, Inc., 2010.

Moss, Wes. *You Can Retire Sooner than You Think*. New York, NY: McGraw Hill Education, 2014.

Nelson, John E., and Richard N. Bolles. *What Color Is Your Parachute? For Retirement, Planning a Prosperous, Healthy, and Happy Future*. New York, NY: Ten Speed Press, an imprint of the Crown Publishing Group, a division of Random House, Inc., 2007.

Newhouse, Meg Ph.D. *Legacies of the Heart: Living a Life that Matters.* Columbia, SC: Ebook Bakery Books, 2016.

Ornish, Dean, M.D. *Love & Survival: 8 Pathways to Intimacy and Health.* New York, NY: HarperCollins Publishers, 1998.

Pascale, Bob, with Louis H. Primavera and Rip Roach. *The Retirement Maze: What You Should Know Before and After You Retire.* Lanham, Maryland: Rowman & Littlefield Publishers, 2012.

Pauley, Jane. *Skywriting: A Life out of the Blue.* New York, NY: Random House, 2004.

Perls, Thomas T., M.D., and Margery Hutter Silver, Ed.D, with John F. Lauerman. *Living to 100: Lessons in Living to Your Maximum Potential at Any Age.* New York, NY: Basic Books, a member of the Perseus Books Group, 1999.

Phipps, Melissa. *The Retirement Rescue Plan: Retirement Planning Solutions for the Millions of Americans Who Haven't Saved Enough.* Berkeley, CA: Sonoma Press, 2016.

Pink, Daniel H. *Free Agent Nation: The Future of Working for Yourself.* New York, NY: The Hachette Book Group, 2001.

Pink, Daniel H. *Drive: The Surprising Truth about What Motivates Us.* New York, NY: Riverhead Books, 2009.

Pollan, Stephen M., and Mark Levine. *Die Broke: A Radical, Four-Part Financial Plan to Restore*

Your Confidence, Increase Your Net Worth, and Afford You the Lifestyle of Your Dreams. New York, NY: HarperBusiness, a division of HarperCollins Publishers, 1997.

Putnam, Robert D. *Bowling Alone: The Collapse and Revival of American Community.* New York, NY: Simon & Schuster Paperbacks, 2000.

Quinn, Jane Bryant. *How to Make Your Money Last: The Indispensable Retirement Guide.* New York, NY: Simon & Schuster Paperbacks, 2016

Rheingold, Stella. *101 Fun Things To Do in Retirement: An Irreverent, Outrageous & Funny Guide to Life after Work.* Sovereign Media Group, 2015.

Roizen, Michael F., M.D., and Mehmet C. Oz, M.D. *You Staying Young: The Owner's Manual for Extending Your Warranty.* New York, NY: Free Press, a division of Simon & Schuster, Inc., 2007.

Roszak, Theodore. 1998. *America the Wise: The Longevity Revolution and the True Wealth of Nations.* Boston, MA: Houghton Mifflin Company, 2007.

Rowe, John W., M.D., and Robert L. Kahn, Ph.D. *Successful Aging: The Surprising Results of the MacArthur Foundation Study—the Most Extensive, Comprehensive Study on Aging in America.* New York, NY: Dell Publishing, 1998.

Schachter-Shalomi, Zalman. *From Age-ing to*

Sage-ing: A Profound New Vision of Growing Older. New York, NY: Warner Books, 1995.

Schlossberg, Nancy K., Ed.D. *Revitalizing Retirement: Reshaping Your Identity, Relationships, and Purpose*. Washington, DC: American Psychological Association, 2009.

Sheehy, Gail. *New Passages: Mapping Your Life Across Time*. New York, NY: A Ballantine Book, published by the Random House Publishing Group, 1995.

Sher, Barbara. *It's Only Too Late If You Don't Start Now: How to Create Your Second Life at Any Age*. New York, NY: Dell Publishing, a division of Random House, Inc., 1998.

Shultz, Kenneth S., Ph.D., with Megan Kaye and Mike Annesley. *Happy Retirement: The Psychology of Reinvention*. New York, NY: Penguin Random House, 2015.

Sightings, Tom. *You Only Retire Once: A Baby Boomer Looks at Health, Finance, Retirement, Grown-up Children…and How Time Flies*. http://sightingsat60.blogspot.com, 2015.

Smith, Hyrum W. *Purposeful Retirement: How to Bring Happiness and Meaning to Your Retirement*. Coral Gables, FL: Mango Publishing Group, a division of Mango Media Inc., 2017.

Solin, Daniel R. *The Smartest Retirement Book You'll Ever Read*. New York, NY: A Perigee Book, the Penguin Group, 2009.

Steinem, Gloria. *Doing Sixty & Seventy*. San Francisco: CA: Elders Academy Press, 2006.

Stone, Howard and Marika. *Too Young to Retire:*

101 Ways to Start the Rest of Your Life. New York, NY: The Penguin Group, 2002.

Strauch, Barbara. *The Secret Life of the Grown-up Brain: The Surprising Talents of the Middle-Aged Mind*. Penguin Books, 2010.

Sterk, Mary CFP. *Ready to Pull the Retirement Trigger*. New York, NY: Morgan James Publishing, 2017.

Taylor, Roberta K. and Dorian Mintzer. *The Couple's Retirement Puzzle: 10 Must-Have Conversations for Creating an Amazing New Life Together*. Naperville, IL: Sourcebooks, Inc., 2014.

Terkeurst, Lysa. *It's Not Supposed to Be This Way*. Nashville, TN: Nelson Books, an imprint of Thomas Nelson, 2018.

Vaillant, George E., M.D. *Aging Well*. New York, NY: Little, Brown and Company, 2002.

Waxman, Barbara, Ed. *How to Love Your Retirement: The Guide to the Best of Your Life*. Atlanta, Georgia: Hundreds of Heads Books, LLC, 2006.

Weil, Andrew, M.D. *Healthy Aging: A Lifelong Guide to Your Well-Being*. New York, NY: Anchor Books, a division of Random House, Inc., 2005.

Wilson, Timothy D. *Redirect: Changing the Stories We Live By*. New York, NY: Back Bay Books / Little, Brown and Company, 2015.

Yeager, Jeff. *How to Retire the Cheapskate Way*. New York, NY: Three Rivers Press, a division of Random House, Inc., 2013.

Zelinski, Ernie J. *How to Retire Happy, Wild, and*

Free: Retirement Wisdom that You Won't Get from Your Financial Advisor. Edmonton, AB, Canada: Visions International Publishing, 2016.

Zimbardo, Philip, and John Boyd. *The Time Paradox: The New Psychology of Time That Will Change Your Life.* New York, NY: Free Press, a division of Simon & Schuster, Inc., 2008.

SOURCES: ARTICLES

American Cancer Society. "Physical Activity and the Cancer Patient." https://www.cancer.org/treatment/survivorship-during-and-after-treatment/staying-active/physical-activity-and-the-cancer-patient.html. Accessed April 2019.

Ashford, Kate. "Horror Stories: When You Die Without A Will." *Forbes.* https://www.forbes.com/sites/kateashford/2016/06/30/no-will/#2a431a982f20. June 30, 2016. Accessed October 2018.

Average Monthly Social Security Benefits, 1940-2015. https://www.infoplease.com/business-finance/us-economy-and-federal-budget/average-monthly-social-security-benefits-1940-2015.

Bellah, Mike. "The Expectation Effect." Our Best Years. http://www.bestyears.com/expectations.html. Accessed October 2018.

Bellah, Mike. "The Myth of Normalcy." Our Best Years.

http://www.bestyears.com/normal.html. Accessed October 2018.

Brandon, Emily. "The Best Places to Retire in 2019." U.S. News and World Report. https://money.usnews.com/money/retirement/slideshows/the-best-places-to-retire. October 10, 2018.

Campbell, Todd. "How Big Is the Average Person's Social Security Check?" The Motley Fool. https://www.fool.com/retirement/2017/08/30/how-big-is-the-average-persons-social-security-che.aspx. Accessed October 2018.

Chen, Michael A., MD. "Being Active When You Have Heart Disease." https://medlineplus.gov/ency/patientinstructions/000094.htm. Accessed April 2019.

Connolly, Kate "When Retirement Takes You by Surprise." http://www.bbc.com/news/world-us-canada-11290776. Accessed October 2018.

Daily, Lyle. "You Won't Believe How Many Baby Boomers Have No Retirement Savings." The Motley Fool. https://www.fool.com/the-ascent/banks/articles/you-wont-believe-how-many-baby-boomers-have-no-retirement-savings/. January 25, 2019. Accessed April 2019.

Davidson, Liz. "The History of Retirement Benefits." http://www.workforce.com/2016/06/21/the-history-of-retirement-benefits/. June 21, 2016. Accessed October 2018.

Emmons, Robert. "Why Gratitude Is Good." https://greatergood.berkeley.Edu/article/item/why_gratitude_is_good [URL inactive]. Accessed October 2018.

Epperson, Sharon. "Retirement May Be Dicey for Single Women." https://www.cnbc.com/2016/03/18/women-more-likely-than-men-to-retire-poor.html. March 22, 2016. Accessed October 2018.

"Gertrude Janeway, 93, Is Dead; Last Widow of a Union Soldier." Associated Press. The New York Times online.

https://www.nytimes.com/2003/01/21/us/gertrude-janeway-93-is-dead-last-widow-of-a-union-soldier.html, January 21, 2003. Accessed October, 2018.

Hannon, Kerry. AARP. "Great Jobs for Workers over 50." https://www.aarp.org/work/working-after-retirement/info-2015/great-jobs-for-50-plus-photo.html#slide1. Accessed April, 2019.

"How to Plan for Rising Health Care Costs." Fidelity. https://www.fidelity.com/viewpoints/personal-finance/plan-for-rising-health-care-costs. Accessed April 1, 2019.

Holmes, Thomas and Richard Rahe. 1967. "The Social Readjustment Rating Scale." *Journal of Psychosomatic Research*. Volume 11, Issue 2, August 1967, 213-218.

Jones, Jeffrey M. "Majority in U.S. Do Not Have a Will." Gallup. https://news.gallup.com/poll/191651/majority-not.aspx. May 8, 2016. Accessed October 2018.

Kaufman, Scott Barry. "The Will and Ways of Hope: Hope Involves the Will to Get There, and Different Ways to Get There." *Psychology Today*. https://www.psychologytoday.com/us/blog/beautiful-minds/201112/the-will-and-ways-hope [URL inactive]. December 26, 2011. Accessed October 2018.

"Love and Survival." Harper Collins Online. https://www.harpercollins.com/9780060930202/love-and-survival/. Accessed April, 2019.

Mansfield, Duncan. "Civil War Romance Seems Like Only Yesterday to Soldier's Widow, 89." Associated Press. Online. http://articles.latimes.com/1998/sep/13/news/mn-22216, September 13, 1998. Accessed October, 2018.

Mayo Clinic Staff. "Exercise: A Drug-Free Approach to Lowering High Blood Pressure." https://www.mayoclinic.org/diseases-conditions/high-blood-pressure/in-depth/high-blood-pressure/art-20045206. Accessed April 2019.

Sources: Articles

"Meades Getting Settled in New Sun City Arizona Community. *Mason City, Iowa, Globe-Gazette*, January 30, 1962, 14. Accessed October 2018.

"Money Scams and Fraud." AARP. https://www.aarp.org/money/scams-fraud/. Accessed April, 2019.

Obrien, Elizabeth. "Retirement Planning for Singles: 5 Tips for Flying Solo." *Time*. http://time.com/money/collection-post/4542729/retirement-planning-for-singles/. 2016. Accessed October 2018.

Osher Lifelong Learning Institutes (OLLI). The Bernard Osher Foundation. http://www.osherfoundation.org/index.php?olli. Accessed October 2018.

Peddicord, Kathleen. "The 10 Best Affordable Places to Retire Overseas in 2019." U.S. News and World Report. https://money.usnews.com/money/retirement/baby-boomers/slideshows/the-best-affordable-places-to-retire-overseas. December 17, 2018.

"A Place in the Sun." *Time*. August 3, 1962. http://content.time.com/time/magazine/article/0,9171,896472,00.html. Accessed October, 2018.

Ramsey, Dave. "A Zero-Based Budget: What and Why." https://www.daveramsey.com/blog/zero-based-budget-what-why. Accessed October 2018.

Reed, Eric. "What Are Average Retirement Savings in 2019?" The Street. https://www.thestreet.com/retirement/average-retirement-savings-14881067. March 3, 2019. Accessed April 2019.

Ring, Wilson. "Meet Ida May Fuller, Recipient of 1st Social Security Check 75 Years Ago." Associated Press. https://www.washingtontimes.com/news/2015/jan/30/ida-may-fuller-was-recipient-1st-social-security-c/. January 30, 2015. Accessed October 2018.

Road Scholar Lifelong Learning Institute. https://www.

roadscholar.org/about/lifelong-learning-institutes/ [URL inactive]. Accessed October 2018.

Rowan, Lisa. "Senior Citizens Can Go to College for Free or Cheap in All 50 States." The Pennyhoarder. November 2, 2016. https://www.thepennyhoarder.com/life/college/free-college-courses-for-senior-citizens/. Accessed October 2018.

Ruffenach, Glenn. "The Biggest Surprises in Retirement." Journal Reports: Wealth Management. *The Wall Street Journal.* https://www.wsj.com/articles/the-biggest-surprises-in-retirement-1486955341. February 12, 2017. Accessed April 2019.

Sarter, Michael. "Public Sector Jobs in States Where the Most People Work for the Government." Bureau of Labor Statistics. USA Today. https://www.usatoday.com/story/money/economy/2018/06/01/states-where-the-most-people-work-for-government/35302753/. Accessed June 1, 2018.

Snyder, C. R., et. al. "The Adult Trait Hope Scale 1991." Positive Psychology Tests and Measures. https://booksite.elsevier.com/9780123745170/Chapter%203/Chapter_3_Worksheet_3.4.pdf. Accessed October 2018.

Social Security Benefits Planner: Retirement. http://www.ssa.gov. Accessed April 2019.

Social Security History. Social Security Website. https://www.ssa.gov/history/imf.html. Accessed October 2018.

Steverman, Ben. "Working Past 70: Americans Can't Seem to Retire. U.S. Seniors Are Employed at the Highest Rates in 55 Years." Bloomberg. https://www.bloomberg.com/news/articles/2017-07-10/working-past-70-americans-can-t-seem-to-retire. 2017. Accessed October 2018.

Strauss, Karsten. "Marc Freedman: Helping Others Find Passion, Purpose and a Paycheck with an Encore." Forbes. https://www.forbes.com/sites/karstenstrauss/2015/08/24/

marc-freedman-helping-others-find-passion-purpose-and-a-paycheck-with-an-encore/#4ca7f63f2712. August 24, 2015. Accessed October, 2018.

Sun City Arizona History. http://suncityaz.org/discover/history/

http://content.time.com/time/magazine/article/0,9171,896472,00.html. Accessed October, 2018.

Wilson, Reid. "More Americans Are Living Alone after the Recession." https://thehill.com/homenews/state-watch/355122-more-americans-are-living-alone-after-recession. Accessed October 2018.

Yenigun, Sami. "Play Doesn't End with Childhood: Why Adults Need Recess Too." National Public Radio. All Things Considered. https://www.npr.org/sections/ed/2014/08/06/336360521/play-doesnt-end-with-childhood-why-adults-need-recess-too. Accessed April 2019.

"You Can't Make Old Friends." Wikipedia. https://en.wikipedia.org/wiki/You_Can%27t_Make_Old_Friends. Accessed Octoberr, 2018.

ACKNOWLEDGMENTS

Many people made this book possible. Writer Mark Williams (who is the most creative person I know) gave initial direction and encouragement. As I tell students, no one knows what he has written until someone tells him, and first readers do that for me. My thanks to Steve Beckham, Sheryl Bullock, John and Sally Carmen, Galen Chandler, Marianne Hammerschmidt, Crystal Harriman, Mike Haynes, Stuart Hughes, Dr. Michael Lee, Joe and Babs Lombard, Gerry and Darla Nickell, Debbie Ortega, Marlene Prigel, and Pam Williamson who all read the initial drafts and gave invaluable feedback.

A good editor can make one look better that he is, and I have Becky Easton, Marlene Prigel, and Kate Beckham to thank for that. My friend and fellow author Rich Bullock showed me the ropes of self-publishing and nursed this work through every step of the process, including doing the internal page design. My gratitude to him is immeasurable. Rob Henslin designed the beautiful cover. I hope his work will inspire readers as much as it did me, and spur them to ask, *What if...?*

Most nonfiction books have subject specialists who help the author with unfamiliar content. Steve Beckham, Stuart Hughes and Lois Ferrara did this for me.

Finally, my wife, Charlotte, is always my first, first reader. Her love is more than I deserve, and without her, I'd still be on that apartment floor.

ABOUT THE AUTHOR

Mike Bellah received a Bachelor of Theology degree from Dallas Bible College in 1973, a M.A. in English Literature from West Texas A & M University in 1995, and a Ph.D. in Technical Communication and Rhetoric from Texas Tech University in 1998. Bellah has worked as a Christian camp director, a pastor, and, from 1993 to his retirement in 2016, he was a college English teacher. As a professor at Amarillo College, Dr. Bellah taught Composition, Technical Writing, Creative Writing, and a continuing education course on *C. S. Lewis' Chronicles of Narnia*. In 2013, he was honored with Amarillo College's highest teaching award, the John F. Mead Faculty Excellence Award. In 2015, the local PBS station selected Dr. Bellah as one of four American Graduate Outstanding Educators.

Bellah's 1988 book, *Baby Boom Believers* (Tyndale House), was a finalist for a Christian Booksellers Association Gold Medallion Award. From 1994-2000 he wrote "Midlife Moments," a weekly column in the *Amarillo Daily News*. After publishing *I Saw Jesus This Morning* in 2009, in 2011 Bellah released his memoir, *Bicycling Through the Midlife Crisis*. Bellah is an avid reader, bicyclist and hiker. Mike and Charlotte Bellah built their retirement home near Canyon, Texas in 2016. In 2018, they celebrated their 50th wedding anniversary. The Bellahs have 5 children and 10 grandchildren.

Ouray, Colorado, 2017

- Do your retirement dreams seem unreachable?
- Are you frustrated by one-size-fits-all approaches that don't work?
- Do you need a step by step plan to get started?

The most important story you will read on retirement is not mine; neither is it one written by any other author. The most important story you will read is *your* story, the one you will write, the one that will shape you as you shape it, the one that will help make your dreams come true. ***Write your's now!***

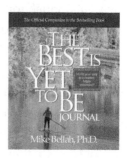

– *The Best Is Yet To Be Journal* – Available on Amazon